OUT OF THE CAGE

A Complete Guide To Beating
A Mixed Martial Artist
On The Street

by
Sammy Franco

Other Books by Sammy Franco:

Heavy Bag Training: Boxing - Mixed Martial Arts - Self Defense
Gun Safety: For Home Defense and Concealed Carry
Warrior Wisdom: Inspiring Ideas from the World's Greatest Warriors
Feral Fighting: Level 2 Widow Maker Program
The Combat Conditioning Workout Journal
War Blade: A Complete Guide to Tactical Knife Fighting
The Widow Maker Program: Maximum Punishment for Extreme Situations
War Craft: Street Fighting Tactics of the War Machine
War Machine: How to Transform Yourself into a Vicious and Deadly Street Fighter
The Bigger They Are, The Harder They Fall: How to Defeat a Larger & Stronger Adversary in a Street fight
First Strike: Mastering the Pre-Emptive Strike for Street Combat
1001 Street Fighting Secrets: The Principles of Contemporary Fighting Arts
When Seconds Count: Everyone's Guide to Self-Defense
Killer Instinct: Unarmed Combat for Street Survival
Street Lethal: Unarmed Urban Combat

Out of the Cage: A Complete Guide To Beating A Mixed Martial Artist On The Street

Copyright 2013 by Sammy Franco
ISBN 978-0-9890382-0-1
Printed in the United States of America
This book is also available in Kindle and iBook formats.

Published by Sammy Franco
Contemporary Fighting Arts, LLC.
P.O. Box 84028
Gaithersburg. Maryland 20883
United States of America
Toll Free: 1 877-232-3334

Direct inquiries and/or orders to the above address.
Neither the author nor the publisher assumes any responsibility for the use or misuse of information contained in this book.

Book concept and photo selection by Sammy Franco
For author interviews, or other publicity information, please send inquiries in care of the publisher or visit the CFA web site at: www.contemporaryfightingarts.com

"A street fight is the ultimate "no holds barred fight" that often has deadly consequences."

- Sammy Franco

Contents

Warning!

The techniques, tactics, methods, and information described and depicted in this self defense book can be dangerous and could result in serious injury and or death and should not be used or practiced in any way without the guidance of a professional CFA instructor.

The author, publisher, and distributors of this book will accept no responsibility, nor are they liable to any person or entity whatsoever for any injury, damage, or loss of any sort that may arise out of practicing, teaching, or disseminating of any techniques or ideas contained herein. This book is about an art form and should be viewed as such. This text is for academic study only.

The author and distributor does not intend for any of the information contained in this book to be used for criminal purposes.

Additionally, it is the reader's responsibility to research and comply with all local, state, and federal laws and regulations regarding the topics covered in this self defense book.

Before you begin any exercise program, including those suggested in this book, it is important to check with your physician to see if you have any condition that might be aggravated by strenuous exercise.

About This Book

Out of the Cage is designed to provide you with the knowledge, skills and attitudes necessary to escape, counter and defeat a mixed martial artists in a street fight. This book will provide you with numerous tactics and techniques that can be readily applied in a self defense situation. Keep in mind, this book addresses issues related to "real-world" self-defense scenarios, it is not designed for MMA sport combat or no holds barred competitions. What you are about to learn is real!

Beware, some of the information and techniques contained herein are lethal and should only be used to protect yourself or a loved one from the immediate risk of unlawful criminal attack. Remember, the decision to employ physical force must always be a last resort, after all other means of avoiding violence has been thoroughly exhausted.

This book is also a skill-building workbook. So feel free to write in the margins, underline passages, and dog-ear the pages. I strongly recommend that you read this text from beginning to end, chapter by chapter. Only after you have read the entire book, should you treat it like a reference and skip around, reading those sections that interest you.

Finally, since most of the words in this text are defined within the context of Contemporary Fighting Arts and its related elements, I have provided a glossary of terms.

Sammy Franco
Founder and President
Contemporary Fighting Arts

INTRODUCTION

Contemporary Fighting Arts

 Contemporary Fighting Arts® (CFA), is a state-of-the-art combat system that was introduced to the world in 1983. This sophisticated and practical system of self-defense is designed specifically to provide efficient and effective methods to avoid, defuse, confront, and neutralize both armed and unarmed assailants in a variety of deadly situations and circumstances.

Unlike karate, kung-fu and the like, CFA is the first offensive-based American martial art that is specifically designed for the violence that plagues our cruel city streets. CFA dispenses with the extraneous and the impractical and focuses on real-life street fighting.

Every tool, technique and tactic found within the CFA system must meet three essential criteria for fighting: efficiency, effectiveness, and safety. Efficiency means that the techniques permit you to reach your combative objective quickly and economically. Effectiveness means that the elements of the system will produce the desired effect. Finally, Safety means that the combative elements provide the least amount of danger and risk for you - the fighter.

CFA is not about mind-numbing tournaments or senseless competition. It does not require you to waste time and energy practicing forms (katas) or other impractical rituals. There are no theatrical kicks or exotic techniques. Finally, CFA does not adhere blindly to tradition for tradition's sake. Simply put, it is a scientific yet pragmatic approach to staying alive on the streets.

CFA has been taught to people of all walks of life. Some include the U.S. Border Patrol, police officers, deputy sheriffs, security guards, military personnel, private investigators, surgeons, lawyers, college professors, airline pilots, as well as black belts, boxers, and kick boxers. CFA's broad appeal results from its ability to teach people how to <u>really</u> fight.

It's All In A Name!

Before discussing the three components that make up Contemporary Fighting Arts, it is important to understand how CFA acquired its unique name. To begin, the first word, "Contemporary," was selected because it refers to the system's modern, up-to-date orientation. Unlike traditional martial arts, CFA is specifically designed to meet the challenges of our modern world.

The second term, "Fighting," was chosen because it accurately describes the system's combat orientation. After all, why not just call it Contemporary Martial Arts? There are two reasons for this. First, the word "martial" conjures up images of traditional and impractical martial art forms that are antithetical to the system. Second, why dilute a perfectly functional name when the word "fighting" defines the system so succinctly? Contemporary Fighting Arts is about teaching people how to really fight.

Let's look at the last word, "Arts." In the subjective sense, "art" refers to the combat skills that are acquired through arduous study, practice, and observation. The bottom line is that effective street fighting skills will require consistent practice and attention. Take, for example, something as seemingly basic as an elbow strike, which will actually require hundreds of hours of practice to perfect.

The pluralization of the word "Art" reflects CFA's protean instruction. The various components of CFA's training (i.e., firearms training, stick fighting, ground fighting, natural body weapon mastery, and so on) have all truly earned their status as individual art forms and, as such, require years of consistent study and practice to perfect. To acquire a greater understanding of CFA, here is an overview of the system's three vital components: the physical, the mental, and the spiritual.

"Contemporary Fighting Arts is about teaching people how to really fight."

The Physical Component

The physical component of CFA focuses on the physical development of a fighter, including physical fitness, weapon and technique mastery, and self-defense attributes.

Physical Fitness

If you are going to prevail in a street fight, you must be physically fit. It's that simple. In fact, you will never master the tools and skills of combat unless you're in excellent physical shape. On the average, you will have to spend more than an hour a day to achieve maximum fitness.

In CFA physical fitness comprises the following three broad components: cardiorespiratory conditioning, muscular/skeletal conditioning, and proper body composition.

The cardiorespiratory system includes the heart, lungs, and circulatory system, which undergo tremendous stress during the course of a street fight. So you're going to have to run, jog, bike, swim, or skip rope to develop sound cardiorespiratory conditioning. Each aerobic workout should last a minimum of 30 minutes and be performed at least four times per week.

The second component of physical fitness is muscular/skeletal conditioning. In the streets, the strong survive and the rest go to the morgue. To strengthen your bones and muscles to withstand the rigors of a real fight, your program must include progressive resistance (weight training) and calisthenics. You will also need a stretching program designed to loosen up every muscle group. You can't kick, punch, ground fight, or otherwise execute the necessary body mechanics if you're "tight" or inflexible. Stretching on a regular basis will also increase the muscles' range of motion, improve circulation, reduce the possibility of injury, and relieve daily stress.

The final component of physical fitness is proper body composition: simply, the ratio of fat to lean body tissue. Your diet and training regimen will affect your level or percentage of body fat significantly. A sensible and consistent exercise program accompanied by a healthy and balanced diet will facilitate proper body composition. Do not neglect this important aspect of physical fitness.

> *"If you are going to prevail in a street fight, you must be physically fit. It's that simple."*

Weapon and Technique Mastery

You won't stand a chance against a vicious assailant if you don't master the weapons and tools of fighting. In CFA, we teach our students both armed and unarmed methods of combat. Unarmed fighting requires that you master a complete arsenal of natural body weapons and techniques. In conjunction, you must also learn the various stances, hand positioning, footwork, body mechanics, defensive structure, locks, chokes, and various holds. Keep in mind that something as simple as a basic punch will actually require hundreds of hours to perfect.

Range proficiency is another important aspect of weapon and technique mastery. Briefly, range proficiency is the ability to fight effectively in all three ranges of unarmed fighting. Although punching range tools are emphasized in CFA, kicking and grappling ranges cannot be neglected. Our kicking range tools consist of deceptive and powerful low-line kicks. Grappling range tools include head-butts, elbows, knees, foot stomps, biting, tearing, gouging, and crushing tactics.

Although CFA focuses on striking, we also teach our students a myriad of chokes, locks, and holds that can be used in a ground fight. While such grappling range submission techniques are not the most preferred methods of dealing with a ground fighting situation, they must be studied for the following six reasons: (1) level of force - many ground fighting situations do not justify the use of deadly force. In such instances, you must apply various non-lethal submission holds, (2) nature of the beast - in order to escape any choke, lock or hold, you must first know how to apply them yourself, (3) occupational requirement- some professional occupations (police, security, etc.) require that you possess a working knowledge of various submission techniques, (4) subduing a friend or relative - in many cases it is best to restrain and control a friend or relative with a submission hold instead of striking him with a natural body weapon, (5) anatomical orientation - practicing various chokes, locks and holds will help you develop a strong orientation of the human anatomy, and (6) refutation requirement - finally, if you are going to criticize the combative limitations of any submission hold, you better be sure that you can perform it yourself.

Defensive tools and skills are also taught. Our defensive structure is efficient, uncomplicated, and impenetrable. It provides the fighter maximum protection while allowing complete freedom of choice for acquiring offensive control. Our defensive structure is based on distance, parrying, blocking, evading, mobility, and stance structure. Simplicity is always the key.

Students are also instructed in specific methods of armed fighting. For example, CFA provides instruction about firearms for personal and household protection. We provide specific guidelines for handgun purchasing, operation, nomenclature, proper caliber, shooting fundamentals, cleaning, and safe storage. Our firearm program also focuses on owner responsibility and the legal ramifications regarding the use of deadly force.

CFA's weapons program also consists of natural body weapons, knives and edged weapons, single and double stick, makeshift weaponry, the side-handle baton, and oleoresin capsicum (OC) spray.

"Range proficiency is the ability to fight effectively in all three ranges of unarmed fighting."

Combat Attributes

Your offensive and defensive tools are useless unless they are used strategically. For any tool or technique to be effective in a real fight, it must be accompanied by specific attributes. Attributes are qualities that enhance a particular tool, technique, or maneuver. Some examples include speed, power, timing, coordination, accuracy, non-telegraphic movement, balance, and target orientation.

CFA also has a wide variety of training drills and methodologies designed to develop and sharpen these combat attributes. For example, our students learn to ground fight while blindfolded, spar with one arm tied down, and fight while handcuffed.

Reality is the key. For example, in class students participate in full-contact exercises against fully padded assailants, and real weapon disarms are rehearsed and analyzed in a variety of dangerous scenarios. Students also train with a large variety of equipment, including heavy bags, double-end bags, uppercut bags, pummel bags, focus mitts, striking shields, mirrors, rattan sticks, foam and plastic bats, kicking pads, knife drones, trigger-sensitive (mock) guns, boxing and digit gloves, full-body armor, and hundreds of different environmental props.

There are more than two hundred unique training methodologies used in Contemporary Fighting Arts. Each one is scientifically designed to prepare students for the hard-core realities of real world combat. There are also three specific training methodologies used to develop and sharpen the fundamental attributes and skills of armed and unarmed fighting, including proficiency training, conditioning training, and street training.

Proficiency training can be used for both armed and unarmed skills. When conducted properly, proficiency training develops speed, power, accuracy, non-telegraphic movement, balance, and general psychomotor skill. The training objective is to sharpen one specific body weapon, maneuver, or technique at a time by executing it over and over for a prescribed number of repetitions. Each time the technique or maneuver is executed with "clean" form at various speeds. Movements are also performed with the eyes closed to develop a kinesthetic "feel" for the action. Proficiency training can be accomplished through the use of various types of equipment, including the heavy bag, double-end bag, focus mitts, training knives, real and mock pistols, striking shields, shin and knee guards, foam and plastic bats, mannequin heads, and so on.

"There are more than two hundred unique training methodologies used in Contemporary Fighting Arts. Each one is scientifically designed to prepare students for the hard-core realities of real world combat."

Conditioning training develops endurance, fluidity, rhythm, distancing, timing, speed, footwork, and balance. In most cases, this type of training requires the student to deliver a variety of fighting combinations for three- or four-minute rounds separated by 30-second breaks. Like proficiency training, this type of training can also be performed at various speeds. A good workout consists of at least five rounds. Conditioning training can be performed on the bags with full-contact sparring gear, rubber training knives, focus mitts, kicking shields, and shin guards, or against imaginary assailants in shadow fighting.

Conditioning training is not necessarily limited to just three- or four-minute rounds. For example, CFA's ground fighting training can last as long as 30 minutes. The bottom line is that it all depends on what you are training for.

Street training is the final preparation for the real thing. Since many violent altercations are explosive, lasting an average of 20 seconds, you must prepare for this possible scenario. This means delivering explosive and powerful compound attacks with vicious intent for approximately 20 seconds, resting one minute, and then repeating the process.

Street training prepares you for the stress and immediate fatigue of a real fight. It also develops speed, power, explosiveness, target selection and recognition, timing, footwork, pacing, and breath control. You should practice this methodology in different lighting, on different terrains, and in different environmental settings. You can use different types of training equipment as well. For example, you can prepare yourself for multiple assailants by having your training partners attack you with focus mitts from a variety of angles, ranges, and target postures. For 20 seconds, go after them with vicious low-line kicks, powerful punches, and devastating strikes.

When all is said and done, the physical component creates a fighter who is physically fit and armed with a lethal arsenal of tools, techniques, and weapons that can be deployed with destructive results.

The Mental Component

The mental component of CFA focuses on the cerebral aspects of a fighter, developing killer instinct, strategic/tactical awareness, analysis and integration skills, philosophy, and cognitive skills.

The Killer Instinct

Deep within each of us is a cold and deadly primal power known as the "killer instinct." The killer instinct is a vicious combat mentality that surges to your consciousness and turns you into a fierce fighter who is free of fear, anger, and apprehension. If you want to survive the horrifying dynamics of real criminal violence, you must cultivate and utilize this instinctive killer mentality.

There are 14 unique characteristics of CFA's killer instinct. They are as follows: (1) clear and lucid thinking, (2) heightened situational awareness, (3) adrenaline surge, (4) mobilized body, (5) psychomotor control, (6) absence of distraction, (7) tunnel vision, (8) fearless mind-set, (9) tactical implementation, (10) the lack of emotion, (11) breath control, (12) pseudospeciation, (13) viciousness, and (14) pain tolerance.

Visualization and crisis rehearsal are just two techniques used to develop, refine, and channel this extraordinary source of strength and energy so that it can be used to its full potential.

Strategic/Tactical Awareness

Strategy is the bedrock of preparedness. In CFA, there are three unique categories of strategic awareness that will diminish the likelihood of criminal victimization. They are criminal awareness, situational awareness, and self-awareness. When developed, these essential skills prepare you to assess a wide variety of threats instantaneously and accurately. Once you've made a proper threat assessment, you will be able to choose one of the following five self-defense options: comply, escape, de-escalate, assert, or fight back.

CFA also teaches students to assess a variety of other important factors, including the assailant's demeanor, intent, range, positioning and weapon capability, as well as such environmental issues as escape routes, barriers, terrain, and makeshift weaponry. In addition to assessment skills, CFA also teaches students how to enhance perception and observation skills.

"Deep within each of us is a cold and deadly primal power known as the killer instinct."

Analysis and Integration Skills

The analytical process is intricately linked to understanding how to defend yourself in any threatening situation. If you want to be the best, every aspect of fighting and personal protection must be dissected. Every strategy, tactic, movement, and concept must be broken down to its atomic parts. The three planes (physical, mental, spiritual) of self-defense must be unified scientifically through arduous practice and constant exploration.

CFA's most advanced practitioners have sound insight and understanding of a wide range of sciences and disciplines. They include human anatomy, kinesiology, criminal justice, sociology, kinesics, proxemics, combat physics, emergency medicine, crisis management, histrionics, police and military science, the psychology of aggression, and the role of archetypes.

Analytical exercises are also a regular part of CFA training. For example, we conduct problem-solving sessions involving particular assailants attacking in defined environments. We move hypothetical attackers through various ranges to provide insight into tactical solutions. We scrutinize different methods of attack for their general utility in combat. We also discuss the legal ramifications of self-defense on a frequent basis.

In addition to problem-solving sessions, students are slowly exposed to concepts of integration and modification. Oral and written examinations are given to measure intellectual accomplishment. Unlike traditional systems, CFA does not use colored belts or sashes to identify the student's level of proficiency.

"If you want to be the best, every aspect of fighting and personal protection must be dissected."

Philosophy

Philosophical resolution is essential to a fighter's mental confidence and clarity. Anyone learning the art of war must find the ultimate answers to questions concerning the use of violence in defense of himself or others. To advance to the highest levels of combat awareness, you must find clear and lucid answers to such provocative questions as could you take the life of another, what are your fears, who are you, why are you interested in studying Contemporary Fighting Arts, why are you reading this book, and what is good and what is evil? If you haven't begun the quest to formulate these important questions and answers, then take a break. It's time to figure out just why you want to know the laws and rules of destruction.

Cognitive Skills

Cognitive exercises are also important for improving one's fighting skills. CFA uses visualization and crisis rehearsal scenarios to improve general body mechanics, tools and techniques, and maneuvers, as well as tactic selection. Mental clarity, concentration, and emotional control are also developed to enhance one's ability to call upon the controlled killer instinct.

The Spiritual Component

There are many tough fighters out there. In fact, they reside in every town in every country. However, most are nothing more than vicious animals that lack self-mastery. And self-mastery is what separates the true warrior from the eternal novice.

I am not referring to religious precepts or beliefs when I speak of CFA's spiritual component. Unlike most martial arts, CFA does not merge religion into its spiritual aspect. Religion is a very personal and private matter and should never, be incorporated into any fighting system.

CFA's spiritual component is not something that is taught or studied. Rather, it is that which transcends the physical and mental aspects of being and reality. There is a deeper part of each of us that is a tremendous source of truth and accomplishment.

In CFA, the spiritual component is something that is slowly and progressively acquired. During the challenging quest of combat training, one begins to tap the higher qualities of human nature. Those elements of our being that inherently enable us to know right from wrong and good from evil. As we slowly develop this aspect of our total self, we begin to strengthen qualities profoundly important to the "truth." Such qualities are essential to your growth through the mastery of inner peace, the clarity of your "vision," and your recognition of universal truths.

"Self-mastery is what separates the true warrior from the eternal novice."

One of the goals of my system is to promote virtue and moral responsibility in people who have extreme capacities for physical and mental destructiveness. The spiritual component of fighting is truly the most difficult aspect of personal growth. Yet, unlike the physical component, where the practitioner's abilities will be limited to some degree by genetics and other natural factors, the spiritual component of combat offers unlimited potential for growth and development. In the final analysis, CFA's spiritual component poses the greatest challenges for the student. It is an open-ended plane of unlimited advancement.

You can learn more about my Contemporary Fighting Arts system by visiting one of our official web sites:

- www.sammyfranco.com
- www.contemporaryfightingarts.com

CHAPTER ONE

Mixed Martial Arts Explored

What Are Mixed Martial Arts?

Before I get into the nuts and bolts of fighting a Mixed Martial Artist on the street, it's important to first understand exactly what are mixed martial arts? For all intents and purposes, mixed martial arts or MMA is a concept of fighting where the practitioner simultaneously integrates a variety of fighting styles into a single method of fighting that can be tested in a regulated full-contact combat sport environment.

Mixed Martial Arts involves both stand up and ground fighting so it employs both striking and grappling techniques from a variety of different martial arts styles such as boxing, submission fighting, catch wrestling, jiu jitsu, judo, thai boxing, karate as well as others styles.

"Mixed martial arts is a concept of fighting where the practitioner simultaneously integrates a variety of fighting styles into a single method of fighting that can be tested in a regulated full-contact combat sport environment."

Mixed martial arts are extremely popular nowadays, but in actuality MMA has been around for a very long time. As a matter of fact, mixed martial arts date back to the Greco-Roman era where the ancient martial art Pankration appeared in the Olympic Games. Many historians agree that the mixed martial arts of ancient Greece are very similar to the mixed martial arts of modern day. However, mixed martial arts of today are considered to be one of the most regulated and controlled sports in the world.

Mixed Martial Arts in the United States

It wasn't until 1993 when mixed martial arts were first introduced to the United States through the Ultimate Fighting Championship (UFC), a mixed martial arts promotional company. The UFC showcased various mixed martial arts athletes fighting each other without weight classes and very few few rules, by boxing standards it was a bloodsport where just about "anything goes". In 1995 United States Senator John McCain called mixed martial arts "human cockfighting," and demanded that MMA be regulated by an athletic commission. Senator McCain's destain for mixed martial arts was well known after his remark, *"MMA appeals to the lowest common denominator in our society."*

Many historians agree that the mixed martial arts of ancient Greece are very similar to the mixed martial arts of modern day.

Mixed martial arts "no holds barred" reference would eventually come to an end with the implementation of specific safety rules and regulations. Despite resistance from politicians and safety regulations, mixed martial arts quickly grew in popularity around the world. Mixed martial arts is now big business! It is now estimated that mixed martial arts events are shown in over 130 countries worldwide. While there are other MMA promotional companies, non have achieved the incredible success of the UFC.

"In 1995 United States Senator John McCain called mixed martial arts "human cockfighting," and demanded that MMA be regulated by an athletic commission."

Mixed Martial Arts Popularity

Mixed martial arts appear everywhere. For example, mixed martial arts events and personalities appear in just about every magazine and newspaper. It also frequently appear in television shows, Xbox games and hollywood movies. As well as reality television shows such as Tapout, The Ultimate Fighter and Caged that focus exclusively on the life of mixed martial arts personalities. Finally, MMA also have their own unique workout gear and clothing line such as Tapout, Bad Boy MMA, Affliction, Cage Fighter and Xtreme Couture. For better or worse, it seems like mixed martial arts has taken over the world.

The Father of Mixed Martial Arts

The concept of mixed martial arts is really nothing new to many members of the eclectic martial arts community. As a matter of fact, Bruce Lee was one of the first martial artist to stylistically integrating various martial arts into his Jeet Kune Do concept.

Essentially, Jeet Kune Do is a mixed martial arts concept for adopting what is useful in a fighting style and rejecting what is useless. According to Lee, *"The best fighter is someone who can adapt to any style, to be formless, to adopt an individual's own style and not following the system of styles."* It's no surprise that Bruce Lee is considered by many people to be the "father of mixed martial arts".

"It's no surprise that Bruce Lee is considered by many people to be the father of mixed martial arts."

In order to get you a bit more acquainted with mixed martial arts, I have included some interesting information about its styles, workouts, equipment training, gear, fighting techniques, prohibited foul techniques and weight divisions.

Mixed Martial Arts Styles

Mixed Martial Arts has a variety of different martial art styles integrated to the sport. MMA includes both stand up (striking) and grappling (ground fighting) martial art styles. More will be discussed in the next chapter. However, some fighting styles that are integrated into MMA might include:

- Western Boxing
- Brazilian Jiu Jitsu
- Karate
- Kickboxing

- Shoot Fighting
- Judo
- Muay Thai Boxing
- Western Wrestling
- Catch Wrestling
- Russian Sambo
- Capoeira

Mixed Martial Arts Workouts

Mixed Martial Arts workouts vary as much as the schools and coaches that teach it. Here is a list of just a few MMA workout designed to build speed, power, strength and endurance:

- heavy bag training
- speed bag work
- punching mitt drills
- double end bag training
- rope skipping
- sparring
- ground and pound dummy training
- kettle bell training
- weight training
- running/sprinting
- body conditioning drills and exercises
- body weight exercises (push ups, pull ups, chin ups,etc)
- controlled clinch drills
- ground fighting sparring
- medicine ball training
- resistance band training
- elevation mask training

- sand bag tossing
- sledgehammer work

Mixed Martial Arts Training Equipment

Mixed Martial arts also requires a considerable amount of training equipment. Here are just a few items used in MMA training:

- heavy bag
- grappling dummy
- punching mitts
- double end bag
- MMA sparring gloves
- head gear for sparring
- shin guards
- elbow and knee pads
- ear guard (prevent cauliflower ears)
- floor mats
- jump rope
- running shoes
- mirror for shadow fighting
- striking shields
- medicine ball
- interval timer or stopwatch
- MMA ring or boxing ring

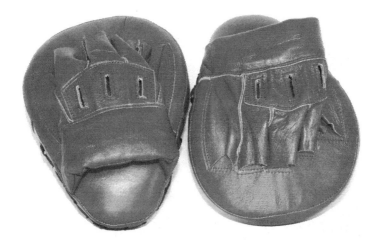

Punching Mitts or "Focus Mitt" training is just a small aspect of MMA training.

Mixed Martial Arts Gear

When you actually participate in a mixed martial arts event, you are required to wear the following items:

- mixed martial art gloves (4 oz.)
- hand wraps
- mouth guards
- mixed martial art shorts
- groin protector "athletic cup"

Just like boxers, mixed martial artists frequently use hand wraps to protect their hands when fighting. However, when it comes to real world self defense, hand wraps are a luxury that will never be available to a reality based self defense technician.

Mixed Martial Arts Kicking Techniques

Here is a brief list of kicking techniques used in mixed martial arts.

- muay thai kick
- front kick
- side kick
- round kick
- jump kick
- flying knee strike

Mixed Martial Arts Clinch Techniques

Here is a brief list of clinch techniques used in mixed martial arts.

- horizontal elbows
- vertical elbows
- knee strikes

Techniques Prohibited in Mixed Martial Arts

The following techniques are just a few techniques that are prohibited in mixed martial arts competition and training. All of them are considered fouls.

- head butting
- eye gouging
- eye raking or any attack to the eyes
- hair pulling
- spitting at the opponent
- biting
- fish hooking
- attacking the groin
- strikes to the back of the head
- striking the spine
- attacking or grabbing the trachea
- breaking fingers or toes
- clawing, pinching or twisting the flesh
- kicking, kneeing or stomping a grounded opponent

Unlike reality based self defense, eye attacks are prohibited in mixed martial arts.

Mixed Martial Arts Weight Divisions

For reasons or safety and fairness mixed martial arts are divided into the following weight divisions.

MMA Flyweight - 125 pounds and under.

MMA Bantamweight - over 125 to 135 pounds

MMA Featherweight - over 135 to 145 pounds

MMA Lightweight - over 145 to 155 pounds

MMA Welterweight - over 155 to 170 pounds

MMA Middleweight - over 170 to 185 pounds

MMA Light Heavyweight - over 185 to 205 pounds

MMA Heavyweight - over 205 to 265 pounds

MMA Super Heavyweight - over 265 pounds

CHAPTER TWO

MMA AND THE STREET

Mainstream Mixed Martial Arts

There's no doubt that mixed martial arts has gone mainstream and it's here to stay. This fact is both good and bad news for you. The good news is, MMA is a clear sign that the world has finally woke up and realized the practicality of integrating combat styles. In essence, the combat arts (by and large) have evolved to a much more functional and respectable level. The days of singular traditional martial art styles and systems are slowly becoming a thing of the past. It's truly evolution in all its glory!

The bad news is, the secret of "stylistic integration" is out of the bag and is no longer insider information to JKD eclectics and Reality Based Self Defense (RBSD) practitioners. Gone are the days when you would most likely face an unseasoned street brawler or traditional or singular style martial artist in a street fight.

Nowadays, just about every Tom, Dick and Harry is practicing some form of mixed martial arts. This is not just limited to law abiding citizens. Believe it or not, there are a lot of bad guys out there studying MMA in an effort to bump up their criminal arsenal. So from this point forward we are all forced to deal with a level playing field.

Mixed martial arts training is not just limited to law abiding citizens, criminals study MMA as well.

"Believe it or not, there are a lot of bad guys out there studying MMA in an effort to bump up their criminal arsenal"

Mixed Martial Arts and Reality Based Self Defense

However, there is some good news! Actually, very good news! While MMA students and fans see the effectiveness of mixed martial arts in the ring they instantly fail to understand its inherent limitations for real world street self defense.

The truth is mixed martial arts (both professional and recreational) are geared exclusively for sport competition and not real world self defense scenarios. In order for mixed martial arts to effectively work in a reality based self defense situation, the following conditions must be present:

- The self defense altercation must be a one on one confrontation.
- Your opponent cannot use weapons such as knives, guns, broken bottles, sticks, etc.
- Your opponent must refrain from using foul techniques such as biting, spitting, groin strikes, finger breaks, head butts, throat crushing, etc.
- Your opponent must be in the same weight class as you.
- Your opponent must be drug free (alcohol, PCP, cocaine must not be present during the confrontation).
- Your opponent must allow you to "tap out" or submit if you feel you are going to get serious injured or choked out.

- Your opponent must give you a one minute rest period so you can regroup and get advice from your coach.

- Your opponent must fight you in a safe and controlled environment such as a boxing ring or octagon cage.

- Your opponent must never attempt to maim, disfigure or kill you.

- You must be able to fight in a safe and familiar environment.

- You can quit fighting or give up anytime you wish without fearing injury or death.

"The truth is mixed martial arts (both professional and recreational) are geared exclusively for sport competition and not real world self defense scenarios."

It's essential that members of both our military and law enforcement realize and understand the inherent dangers and limitations of employing mixed martial arts techniques under "real world" combat conditions. Remember, what works in a "sporting environment" might just get you killed in the real world.

Mixed martial arts training will not equip police officers with the skills and tactics needed to survive real world street encounters.

I hope you get my point. The truth is mixed martial arts have numerous technical and tactical deficiencies for real world self defense applications. This is especially true for law enforcement and military personnel.

However, please don't get me wrong, I have a tremendous amount of respect for mixed martial arts fighters. They are some of the best conditioned athletes in the world and their sport requires a tremendous amount of discipline and hard work. But the truth is, surviving a criminal assault in the streets requires a completely different form of training and a unique mind set.

As a matter of fact, several years ago I actually wrote a tongue-in-cheek article illustrating the drastic differences between mixed martial arts competition and reality based self defense. The article was called, ***"Sammy Franco's Open Challenge"*** and I've included it for you to read.

Mixed martial arts has numerous technical and tactical deficiencies for real world self defense applications. Surviving a criminal assault in the streets requires a completely different set of tools, tactics and techniques coupled with a unique mind set.

Sammy Franco's Open Challenge

"This article is written to clarify some misleading information scattered across the internet regarding Contemporary Fighting Arts and myself. One issue in particular is my open door challenge that is often referred to as "Sammy Franco's Open Challenge". For those of you who are not aware, I posted this open challenge several years ago in response to a few individuals who challenged me to fight under their mixed martial arts (MMA) sport rules.

While I am flattered that some people want to "test their mettle" with me I'm surprised they don't get what I am all about. I have been practicing reality based self defense all my life. I have never been interested in sport combat. While sport combat might entice some people, it just doesn't interest me. It never has! I am all about reality based self defense. This is what I have done all my life and what I will continue to do. But I digress, my open challenge was never intended to recruit a challenger or disparage any style or method of fighting. It was simply designed to illustrate two key points:

1. A reality self defense practitioner has a clear disadvantage when challenged to fight under the mixed martial arts sport rules.

2. There are distinct differences between reality based self defense and MMA sport combat training.

Because of the anonymity of the internet, it becomes a safe haven for idiots, deceivers and nut jobs. A few internet trolls have actually taken my open challenge literally while others have taken it completely out of context. Some people have actually altered and fabricated my words in hopes of inciting anger and hostility. With that being said, here is my open challenge for you to read and make your own logical decision.

Here is the Challenge!

If you challenge me to a fight you must agree to the following terms:

1. You must sign a detailed waiver and release absolving me of any criminal or civil liability in the event of your death. This signature will be observed by three witness and then notarized.

2. There will only be only one rule in my open challenge - there are no rules! This is not a BJJ challenge or an ego driven "my style is better than your style" match. My objective in our fight is simple - I'll do anything and everything to injure, kill or severely cripple you. When I say, no rules, I mean...absolutely no rules. So this means that I can use anything from a knife to a kitchen sink to destroy you. I can also have my friends work you over with baseball bats when we are both locked up on the ground or if I get tired I can just pull out my 9mm and blow your brains out. No rules!

3. If you lose the fight you must pay me $10,000 dollars.

I Agree....It's Insane!

I am sure most of you immediately realize the sheer lunacy of my open challenge. Frankly, only an insane person would willingly accept it. Perhaps, my sardonic request to sign a detailed waiver or the $10,000 fee gave it away. Yes, my open challenge is both ridiculous and somewhat paradoxical. But it illustrates a very important point, the rules of my open challenge are predicated on the nature and characteristics of a real world self defense situation - meaning there are no rules!

As I have stated in many of my books and dvds, street fighting is defined as "a spontaneous and violent confrontation between two or more individuals wherein no rules apply. The operative words are "no rules apply". Ironically, every day law abiding citizens are forced to accept this type of open challenge when they are attacked by a criminal predator.

My point is this! If a mixed martial artist can approach me with a challenge predicated specifically on the nature and characteristics of his training (i.e., sport fighting competition with rules), why can't I do the very same thing to him? Meaning, why can't I offer a counter challenge suggesting we fight under the nature and characteristics of my training (i.e., street fighting with no rules).

An Analogy
Consider this analogy, a mixed martial arts fighter who challenges a reality self defense practitioner to fight under sport rules is like a Ford Mustang challenging a Jeep to a drag race. Conversely, a reality self defense practitioner who challenges a MMA sport fighter to fight by no rules is likened to a Jeep challenging a Mustang to a rock crawling competition. While both vehicles share similar components (i.e., tires, engine, brakes, steering wheel, etc.) they are specifically designed to function in completely different environments and perform much different tasks.

In the final analysis, a mixed martial artist trains to win sport competitions, while self defense practitioners trains to survive an open challenge known as a street fight."

Sammy Franco
Contemporary Fighting Arts

"The rules of my open challenge are predicated on the nature and characteristics of a real world self defense situation - meaning there are no rules!"

Unlike our mean city streets, a mixed martial artist is accustomed to a safe and supportive environment when he is waging war with his adversary.

CHAPTER THREE

The Primary MMA Disciplines

The Five Primary Disciplines of MMA

Now that you have a basic understanding of mixed martial arts and how it differs from the demands of real world street self defense, it's time to delve a bit deeper into MMA. Since a mixed martial artist isn't bound to any singular style or system, he or she can integrate any martial art discipline into their fighting method. However, there are five primary combat disciplines that encompass most mixed martial arts arsenals. They include the following:

- Boxing
- Kickboxing
- Wrestling
- Judo
- Jiu-Jitsu

Boxing

MMA fighters must have a stand up game. They must have the ability to deliver punishing punching range blows against their opponent. From a defensive perspective, they must be able to slip, duck and bob and weave against an oncoming attack. Western boxing skills provide the complete package allowing them to "hold their own" when standing toe-to-toe with an opponent. The boxing arsenal includes the following techniques:

- jab
- straight right
- left and right hooks
- upper cuts
- shovel hooks
- overhand right

"Since a mixed martial artist isn't bound to any singular style or system, he or she can integrate any martial art discipline into their fighting method."

Western boxing techniques play a vital role in MMA.

"Western boxing skills provide the complete package allowing them to "hold their own" when standing toe-to-toe with an opponent."

The Jab   *Straight Right Punch*

Just like the sport of Boxing, two of the staple punches found in a MMA fighter's arsenal is the jab and the straight right punch (aka rear cross punch). When facing a mixed martial artist in punching range you will most likely defend against these two punches.

Kickboxing

Boxing alone will not prepare the MMA fighter for stand-up combat. He must also have a variety of kicking techniques to make his stand-up game complete. In most cases, MMA fighters will add some variation of Muay Thai kickboxing to their fighting method. Muay Thai seems to be the "go to" kickboxing style because it provides the MMA fighter with an extremely powerful offensive arsenal. Thai kickboxing also teaches MMA fighters how to effectively control the opponent's body through aggressive neck clinching techniques. Some of the Muay Thai kickboxing techniques includes:

- front kick (low, mid and high line)
- round kicks (low, mid and high line)
- elbow strikes
- knee strikes

"Boxing alone will not prepare the MMA fighter for stand-up combat. He must also have a variety of kicking techniques to make his stand-up game complete."

Keep in mind that kickboxing techniques are not just limited to the popular style of Muay Thai. There are also countless kickboxing methods and styles that can be integrated with a MMA fighting method. This means some of the following technique might also be present in his arsenal, including some of the following:

- side kick (mid line and high line kicks)
- spinning kicks of all sorts (mid line and high line)
- crescent kicks (mid line and high line)
- axe kicks
- flying kicks of all sorts

Believe it or not, flying kicks such as the one featured in this photo are sometimes used by MMA fighters.

Wrestling

Most mixed martial artists will have some foundational training in either freestyle or Greco-Roman wrestling. Wrestling is essential because it provides the fighter with a solid foundation for grappling. Wrestling also provides the MMA fighter with the skill and ability to control the opponent's body movement when the two of them lock up. Most importantly, wrestling also teaches the fighter how to defend against throws and takedowns.

Wrestling is essential component of mixed martial arts because it provides the fighter with a solid foundation for grappling."

Judo

Once a MMA fighter has locked up in the clinch it's vital that he knows how to use his opponent's balance and weight against him. Judo is a martial art style that teaches this skill. In essence, Judo teaches a mixed martial artist how to disrupt and exploit the opponent's balance so he can perform a variety of throws and devastating takedowns.

"Judo teaches a mixed martial artist how to disrupt and exploit the opponent's balance so he can perform a variety of throws and devastating takedowns."

Jiu-Jitsu

For all intents and purposes, Jiu-Jitsu is predominantly used for the inevitable ground fight. Because the Gracie family dominated the UFC in the early years, most MMA fighters will seek out Brazilian Jiu-Jitsu. Brazilian Jiu-Jitsu arms the MMA fighter with some of the following skills and ground fighting techniques:

- arm locks
- shoulder locks
- leg and ankle locks
- choking techniques

Make no mistake about it, Jiu-Jitsu techniques can be found in just about every mixed martial arts arsenal.

CHAPTER FOUR

Understanding MMA Tactics

MMA's Biggest Weapon

While a mixed martial artist has a broad arsenal of techniques that can be deployed in a variety of combat ranges, one of the most important concerns for you is the fact that he's a well skilled "grappler." Essentially, a grappler is a fighter who is proficient at fighting in close quarter combat range or CQC range.

This means the mixed martial artist will have the ability to grab, clinch, tackle, throw or wrestle you to the ground where he can pin you, establish a dominant ground fighting position and neutralize you with either striking techniques or a myriad of submission holds and chokes. Bear in mind that grappling can take place when standing up with your opponent (often referred to as clinching) and when on the ground (known as ground fighting).

As I mentioned earlier, since the arrival of the Ultimate Fighting Championship (UFC) and various other "no holds barred" sporting events, grappling styles have become a substantial component of mixed martial arts training. Singular grappling styles are many and they include some of the following:

- Shootfighting
- Brazilian Jiu-Jitsu
- Judo
- Western Wrestling
- Pankration
- Russian Sambo
- Greco-Roman Wrestling
- Vale Tudo
- Pitfighting
- Catch Wrestling

"While a mixed martial artist has a broad arsenal of techniques that can be deployed in a variety of combat ranges, one of the most important concerns for you is the fact that he's a well skilled grappler."

Keep in mind that grappling is not just limited to the MMA fighter. As a matter of fact, less skilled fighters can also pose a substantial threat to you in a violent self defense altercation. For example, the drunken bum, a seasoned street punk, an enraged white-collar worker, or a friend who had too much to drink can employ grappling techniques. Regardless of whom you are faced with, one thing is for certain – all grapplers can pose serious problems for you.

MMA Fighting Tactics

Understanding the mindset and tactics of a skilled MMA fighter is the first step toward learning how to defeat him in a violent self defense altercation. While I can't guarantee how each and every mixed martial artist will fight in a violent self defense altercation, there are, however, several predictable tactics that are instilled in most MMA fighters and will most likely be present. You must be cognizant of the "tactics" and be prepared to counter them without apprehension.

It's All About Grappling

For all intents and purposes, a mixed martial artist ultimate objective in a fight is to close the distance gap and maintain a grappling range where he can deliver a variety of close quarter combat strikes and techniques. Fighting in the grappling range of unarmed combat has several advantages for the MMA fighter and they include the following:

1. **Grappling is an Enigma to the Layperson** - Grappling is a very sophisticated form of unarmed combat that very few people truly understand. In fact, the average martial artist is ill prepared for a grappling and ground fighting situation. Once the uninitiated is locked up in a clinch or taken to the ground, it is just a matter of a few moments before he is completely helpless and overwhelmed with panic.

2. **Grappling Range is Inevitable** - Since striking (with legs, fists, elbows, etc) is predicated on forward movement, it's almost certain that two fighters will inevitably collide into one another, clinch and lock-up. It's simply the dynamics of combat. Perhaps this explains why ninety percent of all fights end up in the clinch or the ground. Moreover, many self-defense confrontations often begin at close-quarter or grappling range.

3. **Grappling is Easy to Maintain** - Because of its close proximity and maximal body entanglement, grappling range is the easiest distance to maintain and do damage. Unlike kicking and punching ranges, grapplers do not have to worry about breaking their hands when punching or missing a target when kicking. Once the grappler gets a hold of you, he has you. Period!

4. **It's Familiar and Comfortable** - Grappling range or close quarter combat range provides a feeling of "combat familiarity" for the MMA fighter. In most cases, he will go where "it's relatively safe and comfortable" to him.

Statistically speaking, the "average joe" might be able to throw a punch or kick in a fight, but when it comes to grappling range, he is oblivious.

Unlike most street fighters and traditional martial artists, the mixed martial artist prefers to fight on the ground. The ground is a relatively safe and comfortable environment for him to fight.

An MMA Probable Method of Attack

With that being said, here is an example of how a mixed martial arts fighter might approach a street fight. Once again, this is just an example and not necessarily the rule!

1. The MMA fighter might start off by probing you with jabs or linear kicks to either set you up or get a feel for your overall reaction time.

2. At the ideal moment, he might close the distance gap, striking or "checking" you as he moves into close quarter combat range.

3. Once in close quarter range, he would clinch and grab hold of you.

4. Once he is "locked up" with you in the clinch, he will either deliver more CQC strikes or take you to the ground where he can establish a dominant ground fighting position.

5. From the dominant ground fighting position he can either attack with a flurry of punches or submission locks and chokes.

Once an MMA fighter closes the distance gap, he will most likely lock up in a clinch or take you to the ground. In this photo, the MMA fighter on the right delivers a knee strike from the clinch position.

The Four Essential MMA Attributes

In order for a mixed martial artist to "grapple" effectively, he must have a variety of grappling techniques in his arsenal as well as four essential attributes. Attributes are qualities that enhance his combat technique. Let's take a look at each one.

- Timing
- Kinesics
- Patience
- Deception

Timing

A mixed martial artist has an excellent sense of timing. They can measure distance accurately and they know how to gauge distance with time. What this means is, a well seasoned MMA grappler knows exactly when to rush in or close the distance gap. Once he closes this distance gap he will most likely lock up with you in a clinch or take you to the ground where the can unleash his ground fighting arsenal.

Kinesics

Mixed martial artists are keen observers of body language. They can instantly recognize when you are off balance or shifting your weight at a vulnerable moment. This observation skill will allow him to exploit your vulnerability.

Patience

MMA fighters are relatively patient. Contrary to what some people might think, they don't just rush through the ranges of unarmed combat with reckless abandon. Like a predator about to attack his prey, the skilled MMA fighter will patiently stalk the perimeter of engagement waiting for the ideal moment to move in.

Deception

Skilled MMA grapplers are also deceptive. Many often initiate a feint (the movement of a limb that draws an offensive or defensive reaction) or a fake (body movements that illicit an offensive or defensive reaction) prior to rushing in and attacking. This feint or fake is a critical component of their arsenal because it creates a futile and vulnerable reaction from the opponent, which in turn permits him to safely close the distance gap.

> *"Like a predator about to attack his prey, the skilled MMA fighter will patiently stalk the perimeter of engagement waiting for the ideal moment to move in."*

A Chink In The MMA Armor

Many mixed martial artists are oblivious to the inherent dangers of grappling and ground fighting in a self defense altercation on the streets. Many of them quickly forget that our mean city streets are not the safe haven of a spacious boxing ring or octagon cage.

What follows are some of the clear dangers and disadvantages a mixed martial artist might face when grappling or ground fighting on the streets. Pay close attention because this will clearly illustrate the chink in a mixed martial artists armor.

Multiple Opponents

To begin, since grappling and ground fighting requires maximal body entanglement, it is virtually impossible for a MMA grappler to fight multiple attackers at the same time. Remember, on the streets you never know if your opponent has friends that are close by and ready to help out.

Positional Asphyxia

Positional asphyxia is another concern when ground fighting a very large and heavy assailant. In simple terms, positional asphyxia is the arrangement, placement or positioning of your opponent's body which interrupts your breathing and causes unconsciousness or possible death.

Two of the greatest dangers about mixed martial arts grappling and ground fighting are multiple attackers and street weapons. Mixed martial arts training will not prepare you to handle these three guys.

Edged Weapons

It is also very difficult for an MMA grappler to defend against knives and other edged weapons when locked up with his opponent in the clinch or on the ground. Remember, for someone to survive an edged weapon attack, he must be highly skilled and trained under the guidance of a "reality based" self defense expert.

Time Consuming Fighting Method

I have often told my students that ground fighting and some forms of grappling can be a game of "physical chess" requiring patience and time. But the fact is, time is a true luxury in real world combat situations. In most cases, a street fight altercation is over just as quickly as it started.

The bottom line is, on the streets you don't have time to "play chess" and wait for your opponent to make his next move on the ground.

It is very difficult for a mixed martial arts grappler to defend against knives and other edged weapons when locked up with his opponent in the clinch or on the ground.

No Weight Divisions

There's a very good reason why there are specific weight divisions in MMA matches. The fact of the matter is, body weight and somatotypes do play a critical role in the overall effectiveness of grappling and ground fighting techniques.

In a violent street fight, an MMA fighter might have to fight an adversary twice his weight, strength and size. This can and will significantly weaken (if not nullify) the overall effectiveness of his grappling and ground fighting techniques.

When it comes to mixed martial arts grappling and ground fighting, size, bodyweight and strength play a critical role in the outcome of a fight. Never let anyone convince you that "technique alone" makes MMA close quarter combat techniques effective. Would a Welterweight (155 to 170 pounds) mixed martial artist really want to fight the man on the right?

Dangerous Terrain Or Environment

Ground fighting on certain types of terrain can sometimes be hazardous to your health (e.g., broken glass, sharp metal objects, broken or splintered wood, concrete pavement, etc). Your environment and immediate surrounding is another danger when ground fighting (i.e., heavy traffic, a cliff, a street curb, steep hill, marsh, thorn bushes, bridges, etc).

Just about every mixed martial artist is accustomed to performing his fighting techniques in a safe and controlled environment such as a boxing ring or octagon cage. Most are unaware that a street fighting environment can negate the effectiveness of many MMA techniques.

Psychoactive Drugs

If a mixed martial artist is faced with an adversary who is high on psychoactive drugs he will be dealing with an opponent who is freakishly strong and immune to pain. I know of one case where it took five police officers ten minutes to wrestle and arrest a 120-pound woman who was high on PCP. Could you image how difficult it would be for an MMA fighter to fight a large man on such powerful drugs? The bottom line is most mixed martial arts techniques will not work against people who are high on these types of drugs.

Dispelling The MMA Myths

Before I close out this chapter, I'd like to remind you that mixed martial artists are very formidable fighters and should never be stereotyped as ignorant hillbilly wanna-be warriors. Many are serious and intelligent athletes who take their sport very seriously.

To drive my point home, I have included a list of ridiculous myths about MMA fighters that have been promulgated within the martial arts world. Here are ten of the most common ones.

Myth 1: "MMA Fighters Are Not Strategic Fighters."

Untrue! Mixed martial artists are largely shrewd tacticians who can outsmart their opponents. For example, during a ground fight, the grappler is constantly assessing and scrutinizing such important factors like positioning, energy expenditure, weight distribution shifts and reaction dynamics.

Myth 2: "Small MMA Fighters Cannot Grapple or Ground Fight."

While it's true that size, strength and bodyweight play a significant role in the outcome of a self defense situation, it's also true that you don't have to be the size of a professional wrestler to be an effective or dangerous grappler. Small-framed men can move like lightning on the ground and can be extremely dangerous.

Myth 3: "MMA Fighters Don't Really Know How To Punch."

This myth is truly absurd! While most MMA fighters are not striking experts, many of them know how to throw a good punch and are quite capable of pounding you into dust. In fact, many mixed martial artists will readily employ striking techniques to set you up for a takedown, weaken your spirit, or soften you up for a painful submission hold.

Don't be fooled, just about every mixed martial artists knows how to throw a good punch.

Myth 4: "MMA Fighters Are Generally Fat or Out of Shape."

Wrong! Mixed martial artists are some of the best conditioned athletes in the world. Since they spend a considerable amount of time conditioning themselves to absorb tremendous punishment, their bodies are usually muscular and hard. They also possess excellent stamina and endurance, terrific upper body strength, and uncommon gripping strength. Moreover, they are no stranger to pain and discomfort.

Myth 5: "MMA Fighters Need A Uniform or Gi in Order To Fight Well."

This is another ridiculous myth. While there are several martial art styles that train with traditional gi's, I can assure you that MMA fighters are more than prepared to fight without one.

Mixed martial artists are some of the best conditioned athletes in the world.

Myth 6: "You Can Knock-Out An MMA Grappler With One Solid Punch."
This is one of the greatest myths. It is extremely difficult to effectively punch or kick a mixed martial artists or any seasoned fighter who is rushing in or tackling you. Many tough grapplers actually expect to be hit during a take down. They know that a glancing blow will have virtually no effect on them.

Myth 7: "MMA Grapplers Are Slow."
Want to bet! Mixed martial arts grapplers are very fast fighters who can close the distance gap in the blink of an eye. Many of them have extremely powerful legs that can explosively launch them into ranges of engagement.

A grappler may lose approximately 30 percent of his arsenal if both of you are not wearing a uniform or gi, however 70 percent of his grappling arsenal is still readily available.

Myth 8: "You Can End a Ground Fight With One Simple Eye Gouge or Groin Strike."

I have actually heard this foolish statement from several well known self defense experts and they are wrong! Dead wrong! Anyone who has ever experienced real ground fighting knows that it takes a hell of a lot more than a thumb gouge to the eye or groin strike to end a vicious ground fight. Single weapon strikes <u>will not put an end to a combat situation</u>.

Successfully defeating a mixed martial artist on the ground requires a significant amount of knowledge, skill and ground fighting training. There is no way around it! You must know how to ground fight if you want to stand a chance against any mixed martial artist. Period!

Single weapon strikes will seldom put an end to a self defense situation.

Myth 9: "The Odds of Fighting a Mixed Martial Artist On The Streets Are Slim to None."

First, you never know who you will fight on the streets. To assume that you will never face an adversary who has MMA grappling or ground fighting skills is both stupid and naive. Believe me, there are many rogue MMA fighters out there who would love to test their mettle on innocent law abiding citizens.

Second, there is a very strong possibility that you might fight a street punk who knows how to execute the most rudimentary MMA maneuvers or techniques. Just about anyone can execute some type of MMA grappling or wrestling technique in a street fight. Consider how many American youths engage in recreational football only to call upon it in their adult years. Do you know the amount of damage an old fashioned football tackle can do to you in a street fight?

Myth 10: "I Study Mixed Martial Arts, So I Can Protect Myself On The Streets."

Not true! The problem is that mixed martial arts are grossly inadequate for real street combat. Furthermore, many MMA fighters believe that when faced with a real world self defense situation, they will simply grapple with their opponent or take him to the ground and finish him off with submission technique. While this may sound like a good plan, I can assure you that it's dangerous, if not deadly for the MMA practitioner.

This is not to say that all MMA techniques are useless in a self defense situation. Some can actually be effective for the streets. However, to predicate your entire method of combat on mixed martial arts techniques alone can get you severely injured of killed on the streets.

A competent self defense technician must have both stand up and ground fighting skills that are specifically designed for street self defense. This means each and every tool and technique must be efficient, effective and safe. Moreover, a smart self defense technician must also be acutely aware of the limitations and inherent dangers of grappling and ground fighting in the streets.

CHAPTER FIVE

Fighting In The Clinch

As I mentioned in chapter four, your biggest concern when fighting a mixed martial artist is the fact that he's a skilled grappler that can grab, clinch, tackle, throw or wrestle you to the ground.

Now there is some good news and some bad news. First, the bad news. The vast majority of all self defense altercations invariably end up on the ground. So logic dictates there's a very good possibility that you and your MMA opponent will end up on the ground. You will therefore need to arm yourself with a variety of "street functional" ground fighting skills and techniques. Much more will be discussed in chapter seven.

You don't have to be a mixed martial artist or self defense student to realize the vast majority of self defense situations will end up on the ground. Victims of sexual assault are well aware of this sobering fact!

Now, for the good news! Nearly one hundred percent of all violent street altercations will begin from a standing position (i.e., both you and your adversary are standing on your feet). So there's always the possibility that you can end a fight before a mixed martial artist takes you to the ground. Remember this is a strategic possibility and not a guarantee.

Ranges of Combat

Keep in mind that your ultimate objective when fighting a mixed martial artist is to end the street fight before it goes to the ground. This may sound easy, but I can assure that it's not such a simple task. There are several tactics and strategies that must be implemented to ensure your success. However, before I can teach you these techniques and tactics, you must be absolutely certain that you have a clear understanding of the ranges of unarmed combat. Let's first begin with the neutral zone.

Nearly one hundred percent of most violent street altercations will begin from a standing position (i.e., both you and your adversary are standing on your feet). So there's always is the possibility that you can end a fight before a mixed martial artist takes you to the ground.

The Neutral Zone

In unarmed combat, the neutral zone is not a range of combative engagement. It is the distance at which neither you or your opponent can physically strike one another with your limbs. The neutral zone serves a strategic purpose by enhancing your defensive reaction time in the event that your opponent attacks you first. If the MMA fighter elects to rush you from the neutral zone, you will have sufficient reaction time to counter his attack.

Kicking Range

The furthest distance of unarmed combat is kicking range. At this distance you adversary is usually too far away to strike with your hands, so he would use his legs to strike you.

In this photo, a mixed martial artist delivers a thai kick from the kicking range of unarmed combat.

Punching Range

Punching range is the mid-range of unarmed combat. At this distance, your opponent is close enough to strike you with his hands and fists. Punching range techniques can be quick, efficient and effective and they are the foundation of any compound attack.

In this photo, a mixed martial artist stands in front of a heavy bag from the punching range.

Grappling Range

The third and closest range of unarmed combat is the grappling range. At this distance, your MMA opponent is too close to kick or deliver hand strikes, so he would use close-quarter tools and techniques.

Moreover, grappling range is divided into two different planes, vertical and horizontal. In the vertical plane (also know as clinch range), your opponent can deliver impact techniques like elbow and knee strikes. In the horizontal plane of grappling range, both you and your adversary are ground fighting.

In this photo, a mixed martial artist delivers a knee strike from the grappling range of unarmed combat.

Pictured here is the grappling range in the horizontal plane. Note that the man is punching from the top "mounted position".

Understanding the Clinch

Now that you are aware of the three ranges of unarmed combat, you need to know how to fight from the clinch position First, let me explain that clinching occurs in grappling range and it's the process of strategically locking up with your opponent while the two of you are both standing. Keep in mind that clinching in grappling range is a mixed martial artists forte, so you will have your work cut out for you.

Effective clinching skills play a vital role in determining if you end up on the ground with a MMA grappler. So if you want to avoid wrestling on the ground with your adversary then you must know how to fight in the clinch and ultimately control it. Remember, the clinch is the last range of combat before the two of you go to the ground. So if you don't use this golden opportunity to neutralize the mixed martial artist you can bet that the both of you are going to the ground. And the ground is one of the worst places to be when engaged in a street fight.

Interestingly enough, most violent confrontations invariably end up with the two combatants locked up in some sort of temporary clinch. Very seldom is it the result of strategic planning, more often it's the physical residual of two forces fueled by adrenaline and rage who colliding into one another. Whatever its cause, the clinch is a very real element of street combat that must be mastered if you are to defeat a mixed martial artist.

"If you want to avoid wrestling on the ground with your MMA adversary then you must know how to fight in the clinch and ultimately control it."

Did you know that many (pre-contact stage) street altercations begin at grappling or clinching range? The irony is that most people do not have a clue what to do at this distance of engagement. In this photo, the aggressor (left) encroaches upon the defender (right).

Defensive Clinching

Clinching can be used for both offensive and defensive purposes. For defensive purposes, clinching should be employed immediately after you have performed a specific defensive technique such as a block, parry, stiff-arm jam, webbing technique, etc. By defensively clinching, you negate the grappler's ability to maintain his offensive flow. The objective is to bypass his assault and re-establish offensive control.

For example, let's say a mixed martial artist attacks you with an upper body tackle, you immediately negate his attempted takedown with a stiff-arm jam and move into a clinch position to stabilize your balance and establish a dominant inside position. Once in the clinch position, you counter the adversary with a series of head butts, knee strikes and elbows until he is sufficiently neutralized.

How To Stand When Clinching

A strong well-balanced stance is one of the most overlooked elements of proper clinching technique. The sad fact is too many fighters place too little emphasis on their stance when they lock up with their opponents. Keep in mind that if your stance is flawed, your balance will be lost and your clinch will most likely fall to pieces.

To assume the proper stance when clinching with your MMA adversary, blade your feet and body at approximately 45-degrees from the opponent. This moves your body targets back and away from direct strikes but still leaves you strategically positioned to attack. Place your feet approximately shoulder-width apart with both knees bent and flexible. Your body weight must be equally distributed over both feet. Let your bodyweight sink into the ground. Place both of your hands on the back of the opponent's neck, clamp down hard and be certain that your hands overlap each other. Finally, keep your chin slightly angled down. Remember to always be cognizant of your weight distribution when clinching, if you lose your balance, you are screwed!

How To Control The Clinch

Once you establish the clinch position, it is equally important to maintain and control it. The most important aspect of controlling the clinch is to employ the proper hand gripping technique. This type of neck hold is essential. If you can effectively control the opponent's head in the clinch, you will ultimately control his body.

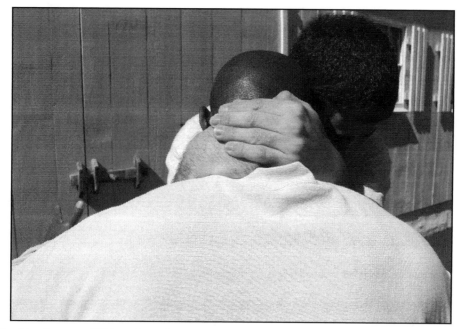

In this photo, a CFA student demonstrates proper hand placement when clinching.

While mixed martial art styles teach a wide variety of clinch positions, in Contemporary Fighting Arts (CFA) there is only one way that really matters in a self defense situation. I refer to it as the "inside position".

To assume the clinch inside position, start by placing both of your hands on the back of the opponent's neck, clamp down hard and be certain that your hands overlap each other. Remember to tuck your elbows in to protect against body shots.

Once your hands secure the opponent's neck, pull down forcefully. Do not just pull with your arms; remember to use your entire body to control him. Also, make certain that both of your forearms run over his collarbone. This will significantly enhance your leverage.

Avoid becoming too tense when clinching with your adversary. You need to be able to feel his weight, balance and energy shift. It's also important not to interlace your fingers when grasping the back of the opponent's neck. Also remember that the inside position is particularly effective against taller MMA opponents.

> *"If you can effectively control the opponent's head in the clinch, you will ultimately control his body."*

How To Beat A Mixed Martial Artist In The Clinch

Once you have established the clinch inside position, it's time to attack your adversary as quickly as possible. It's worth mentioning that a mixed martial artist is trained to have a wider stance when clinching with his opponent. He does this for enhanced stability and to counter possible takedowns, but this sport-oriented posture also leaves his centerline and groin region vulnerable to attack. You must keep this in mind when clinching with him and take advantage of this structural flaw if the opportunity arises.

Use MMA Foul Techniques When Fighting

You must remember that one of the key elements to beating an MMA fighter on the street is to attack him with techniques that he is **NOT** accustomed to defending. Remember the mixed martial arts foul techniques I listed in Chapter One? Well, these are some of the most effective offensive techniques that you can use on your MMA opponent. To refresh your memory I have listed them again:

- head butting
- eye gouging (only in deadly force situations)
- eye raking or any attack to the eyes (only in deadly force situations)
- hair pulling
- spitting at the opponent
- biting (only in deadly force situations)
- fish hooking

- attacking the groin
- strikes to the back of the head (only in deadly force situations)
- striking the spine (only in deadly force situations)
- attacking or grabbing the trachea (only in deadly force situations)
- breaking fingers or toes
- clawing, pinching, ripping or twisting the flesh
- kicking, kneeing or stomping a grounded opponent (only in deadly force situations)

"You must remember that one of the key elements to beating an MMA fighter on the streets is to attack him with techniques that he is NOT accustomed to defending."

But Can't He Use Foul Techniques On Me?

I have also heard some mixed martial artists claim they can and will use the very same foul tactics and techniques against an opponent on the streets, but there is a slight problem with their theory.

The truth is, in order for these MMA foul tactics to work effectively in real world combat conditions, they must be practiced day in and day out until they become an instinctual fighting skill. These techniques must also be added to a variety of reality based self defense (RBSD) drills and full contact exercises, including sparring, ground fighting and simulated street fighting scenarios. Essentially, a mixed martial artist would have to study RBSD to pull it off on the streets!

Use Of Force Option In The Clinch

Now keep in mind that when clinching with your adversary you will have one of two use-of-force options at this point: intermediate use of force and deadly force. Let's take a look at each one.

Intermediate Force - If you are legally and morally justified in using intermediate use of force then you will want to use some of the following offensive tools and techniques in the clinch: Head butts, knee strikes, elbow strikes and certain grappling holds.

Intermediate Force Techniques

What follows are a list of intermediate force techniques that you can use when locked in the clinch with your MMA opponent. They include some of the following:

- Head Butt
- Foot stomp (under specific conditions)
- Horizontal elbow strikes
- Vertical elbow strikes
- Vertical knee strikes
- Diagonal knee strikes
- Hair pulling
- Finger breaks
- Palm jolts

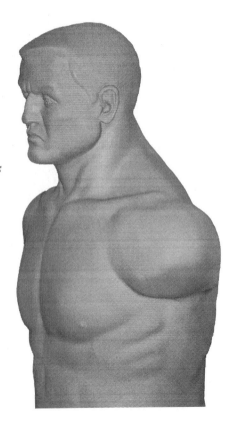

If you don't have the ability to train with a partner, the Body Opponent Bag or BOB is a great tool for working on your clinching techniques.

In this photo, the author delivers a head butt strike from the clinch position. The head butt is classified as an intermediate use of force technique.

"The truth is, in order for these MMA foul tactics to work effectively in real world combat conditions, they must be practiced day in and day out until they become an instinctual fighting skill."

If you don't own a Body Opponent Bag, you can also practice on the heavy bag. In this photo, the fighter delivers a diagonal elbow strike at clinch range.

When you have stabilized your balance and the time is right, you can deliver knee strikes to the opponent's groin and thigh area.

Deadly Force – If you are legally and morally justified in using deadly force then you would either employ our **WidowMaker** or **Savage Street Fighting** methodologies. Let me give you a brief explanation of each one and you can decide if either one is right for you.

The WidowMaker Program

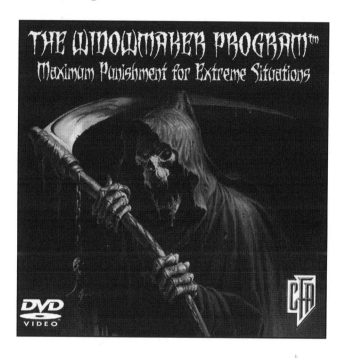

The WidowMaker Program is the foundation of our Razing methodology. Essentially, "razing" is a series of vicious close quarter techniques designed to physically and psychologically extirpate a criminal attacker. These close quarter techniques are executed at various beats. (1/2 beat, 1/4 beat and 0 beat) and they include: eye raking, eye gouging, tearing, crushing, biting, hair pulling, elbow strikes, head butts, bicep pops, neck cranks and finishing chokes.

The WidowMaker Program turns the clinch into a range of deadly engagement. Its unconventional method of attack is absolutely devastating. The WidowMaker Program is for deadly force self defense situations only!

Savage Street Fighting Program

Savage Street Fighting is another extreme combat program designed for close quarter combat range (or CQC range). Savage Street Fighting focuses exclusively on the "zero beat" attack and it must only be used in self defense situations that legally warrant the application of deadly force.

Savage Street Fighting provides the self defense practitioner with one of two possible tactical objectives. First, it forces your adversary to immediately "disengage" or withdraw from fighting you in CQC range. Second, it incapacitates your adversary both physically and mentally.

Just like the WidowMaker Program, Savage Street Fighting is a very unconventional method of combat that is absolutely devastating. You can learn more about both the Widowmaker and Savage Street Fighting programs by visiting my website at www.sammyfranco.com.

Regardless of the level of force you choose to apply when fighting your MMA opponent, it's critical that you are able to recognize the "window of opportunity" within the explosive and unpredictable dynamics of the fight. Once you engage in the clinch, you must immediately attack your opponent with explosive and powerful techniques. Your attack must be overwhelming. This will almost certainly disturb his balance, which in turn will prevent him from leveraging you into a throw or possible takedown.

"Regardless of the level of force you choose to apply when fighting your MMA opponent, it's critical that you are able to recognize the "window of opportunity" within the explosive and unpredictable dynamics of the fight."

The Clinch Swimming Drill

The swimming drill is an excellent exercise for helping you and your partner become acquainted with the clinch as well the proper technique for acquiring the inside position. You will need a training partner to perform this training exercise. Begin with the following steps.

STEP 1: Face your training partner at the grappling range with both of your bodies angled slightly. Stretch you arms forward and place both of your hands on your partner's neck. Have your partner place his arms on the inside of your arms with his hands clasped around your neck (this is known as the "inside position" of the clinch).

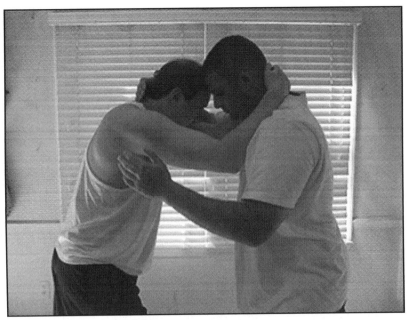

STEP 2: Next, take your left hand off your partner's neck, bring it under and inside his outstretched arm and clasp the back of his neck.

STEP 3: Do the same with your right arm. You will now have the "inside position" and your partner has the outside position. Now it is your training partner's turn to acquire the inside position. Have him follow the same steps that you just performed. Remember to move one arm at a time and use your legs and body to force your training partner backwards as you snake your arms into the inside position. This is a fluid drill, so pay close attention to your form and remain balanced at all times. Once you and your partner get the hang of this swimming motion, you can incorporate various close quarter weapons (i.e., knee strikes, vertical elbows, head butts, etc).

CHAPTER SIX

Countering The Takedown

How To Counter The Takedown

The "takedown" is a staple technique found in just about every MMA fighter's arsenal. For all intents and purposes, a takedown is defined as a technique or maneuver that immediately forces a standing fighter to the floor.

You can be taken down to the floor numerous ways. However, much of it will depend on whom you are fighting. For example, a skilled jiu-jitsu fighter might use a well-executed hip throw while a street punk might attempt a sloppy (but effective) bums rush to take you off your feet.

Also, keep in mind, the type of takedown that your adversary employs can often be influenced by a variety circumstances and factors such as his combat style, state of mind, environment, range and proximity.

In all my years of teaching, I have concluded that regardless of whom you are fighting, your adversary will generally perform a takedown for one of three reasons. They are as follows:

- Strategic Attack
- Desperation Move
- Practitioner Error

Strategic Attack – The takedown is the result of a deliberate and planned method of attack. For example, you and your MMA adversary are fighting in the stand up position; the MMA fighter skillfully defends against your blows, bypasses punching range, clinches with you, and sweeps your feet taking you to the ground.

Desperation Move – You are beating the hell out of the mixed martial artist from the stand up position. He quickly realizes that his stand up fighting skills are grossly deficient and in an act of desperation he grabs hold of you and takes you to the ground.

Practitioner Error – Takedowns are not always pre-meditated, they can be the residual of a mistake or mishap. For example, the mixed martial artist accidentally slips or trips during the course of the stand up fight. He grabs hold of you to stabilize his balance and ends up taking you to the ground with him.

> *"The type of takedown that your adversary employs can often be influenced by a variety circumstances and factors such as his combat style, state of mind, environment, range and proximity."*

The Strategic Attack - Six Ways He Can Take You Down!

A strategic attack can be executed many different ways. There are six strategic takedowns at a MMA fighter's disposal, they are: throwing, tripping, sweeping, locking, striking and body tackles.

Throwing Takedowns - A mixed martial artist arcs your body through the air before it impacts with the floor (i.e. hip throws, fireman's carry, etc.). Throwing takedowns can be deadly! It is often difficult to recover from a violent throw onto the concrete or pavement.

Tripping Takedowns - A mixed martial artist strategically plants his leg and pushes you over it.

Sweeping Takedowns - A mixed martial artist sweeps your foot, or feet, off the ground through a dynamic motion of his leg.

Locking Takedowns - A mixed martial artist locks your joint so he can take you down or throw you down to the floor.

Striking Takedowns - A mixed martial artist strikes you and causes you to fall to the ground. Striking takedowns are the most indirect form of MMA takedowns.

Body Tackles - A mixed martial artist applies pressure or dynamic force (called tackling) to your body or appendage in order to take you down to the ground. Since body tackles are the most common type of takedown used by mixed martial artists, I will focus on them in this chapter.

The Takedown Rule of Thumb

There's a *"Takedown Rule of Thumb"* that most MMA fighters will use in combat. Generally, a mixed martial artist will not attempt to "shoot" for a takedown unless you are within his arm's length. The MMA fighter is well aware that to attempt a takedown beyond his arms reach would be telegraphic and allow you sufficient time to react and counter effectively. Always keep this in mind when squared off with your adversary.

Three Types of Body Tackles

While there are numerous tackles a mixed martial artist might employ in a street fight, you should be familiar with the three standard types. They include the upper body tackle, mid body tackle and lower body tackle. Let's take a look at each one.

Upper Body Tackle - this is also known as the "bum's rush". There's nothing sexy or scientific about this tackle. It is simply a matter of the adversary rushing and grabbing you with a bear hug. It is the momentum of opponent's bodyweight that knocks you off balance and forces you to the ground. Upper body tackles can come from both the front, sides or rear (such as an ambush attack).

In this photo, the Upper Body tackle.

Mid Body Tackle - this is also called a "waist tackle". The mixed martial artist rushes forward, ducks under your arms and tackles you at the waist. Keep in mind that many lay people are skilled at this type of tackle because of recreational football training. Once again, the momentum of the opponent's bodyweight will knock you off balance and take you to the ground.

"Generally, a mixed martial artist will not attempt to "shoot" for a takedown unless you are within his arm's length."

Pictured here, the Mid Body tackle.

Lower Body Tackle - Lower body tackles can come in the form of either "single or double leg" tackles. For example, to perform the single leg tackle, an MMA fighter lowers his base, shoots forward to your lead leg and grabs behind your knee. He then drives his shoulder into your hip and takes you to the ground. Both the single and double leg takedown requires the greatest amount of skill to successfully execute in a street fight.

The Lower Body tackle.

Don't Let Your Opponent Disrupt Your Balance

In order for a mixed martial artist to take you down to the ground, he must first disrupt or "break" your balance. Generally, there are four ways he can accomplish this task. They are the following:

Redirection of Force - This is when your adversary exploits your energy or dynamic pressure and disrupts your balance.

Strength Manipulation - This is when your adversary uses his raw power and sheer strength to disrupt your balance.

Striking Impact - This is when your assailant hits you, causing a reaction dynamic that throws you off-balance.

Feinting or Faking - This is when your assailant feints, draws a defensive reaction from you that throws you off balance.

Striking Impact is one of the four ways you can lose your balance causing you to end up on the ground.

The Stability Drill

The stability drill is excellent for learning how to stabilize your balance once a mixed martial artist has grabbed hold of you. This exercise will also get you accustomed to the critical importance of proper weight shifting by developing your sense of tactile sensitivity.

To begin the drill, square off with your training partner at the grappling range. Then grab hold of each other (you can grab the wrists, elbows, arms, shoulders, the nape of the neck, and waist). Next, have your partner (the designated attacker) initiate the drill by pulling and pushing you in various directions in an effort to throw you off balance.

Grab hold of him and try to stabilize your balance while he is pulling and pushing. Try to quickly adapt to the intense and unpredictable nature of his energy. This drill can get very intense and can last up to five minutes in duration. Advanced self defense practitioners can also perform this exercise while blindfolded.

In this photo, two students perform the stability drill.

You Need A Stance!

Before you can apply the actual defensive moves against a takedown, you will first need a stance. While just about any stance will work with these anti-grappling techniques, one of the best to use is CFA's de-escalation stance.

The De-escalation stance is used during the pre-contact phase of unarmed combat. The proper de-escalation stance (for kicking & punching ranges) can be acquired first blading your body at approximately 45- degrees from the adversary. Then keep both of your feet approximately shoulder-width apart and have your knees slightly bent with your weight evenly distributed. Both of your hands are open, relaxed, and up to protect the upper targets. Keep your torso, pelvis, head, and back erect and stay relaxed and alert - while remaining at ease and in total control of your emotions and body.

Remember to avoid any muscular tension—don't tighten up your shoulders, neck, arms, or thighs (tension restricts breathing and quick evasive movement, and it will quickly sap your vital energy).

The De-escalation Stance.

The takedown defenses featured in this book can also be applied from your basic fighting stance. In this photo, the author demonstrates a left fighting stance.

"Your stance is the foundation for all your anti-grappling techniques."

CFA'S Five Takedown Defenses

Now that you have a rudimentary understanding of the three body tackles and you have a stance, it is time to take the next step and learn takedown defenses. In Contemporary Fighting Arts, we have five different types of takedown defenses. They include the following:

- Range Manipulation
- Height Change to Level of Entry
- Stiff- Arm Jam
- Webbing
- Sprawling

Range Manipulation

As the name implies, range manipulation is the strategic manipulation of combat ranges. If you recall, I mentioned earlier in this chapter that a knowledgeable mixed martial artist will most likely attempt a takedown only if you are within his arms reach (approximately punching range).

Therefore, one of the best ways to delay being taken to the ground is to stay outside of the MMA fighter's "shooting range" with quick and responsive footwork. This will keep the range open and prevent the grappler from setting up an effective takedown. Incidentally, the term "shoot" or "shooting" means an explosive forward movement (generally low level) while grabbing the opponent's legs with the sole objective of taking a person to the ground.

Footwork Basics

The safest footwork for combat involves quick, economical steps performed on the balls of your feet, while you remain relaxed and balanced. When moving on the balls of your feet, always try to keep your legs a shoulder-width apart and your weight evenly distributed. Moving on the balls of your feet does not mean haphazardly dancing around your assailant. This type of "show boating" will get you into serious trouble. Remember to always move with a strategic purpose in mind. Basic footwork is structured around four general directions:

Forward (advance) - from your stance, first move your front foot forward (approximately twelve inches) and then move your rear foot an equal distance.

Backward (retreat) - from your stance, first move your rear foot backward (approximately twelve inches) and then move your front foot an equal distance.

Right (sidestep right) - from your stance, first move your right foot to the right (approximately twelve inches) and then move your left foot an equal distance.

Left (sidestep left) - from your stance, first move your left foot to the left (approximately twelve inches) and then move your right foot an equal distance.

Basic footwork skills should also be practiced from two different states: Static and Ballistic. Static footwork movements are executed from a static or stationary position; while ballistic footwork movements are executed while you are moving.

Do not forget to practice footwork maneuvers with different types of footwear. For example, combat boots, hiking boots, running shoes, dress shoes, cross trainer shoes, sandals, cowboy boots and loafers). In addition, practice footwork skills when you are barefoot.

Range Manipulation Drill

The range manipulation drill is a simple yet effective exercise that will improve your range awareness and sharpen your reflexes.

To perform the drill, have both you and your training partner take turns setting up the takedown while the other quickly opens up the range. Perform this drill for 10 -15 minutes.

Height Change to Level of Entry

A solid and effective takedown will also require your MMA adversary to lower his base and get his hips under you. This means he will have to bend at his knees and back to lower his "level of entry". When your adversary gets within his "shooting range" and lowers his level of entry, it is critical that you can immediately match his height change. This action will dramatically reduce the effectiveness of his takedown.

One of the best weight training exercises for improving your height change reflexes is the squat. The squat is a fantastic exercise that builds mass and strength in the thighs. To perform the exercise do the following:

1. With you feet approximately shoulder width apart and in front of your hips, rest a barbell across the back of your shoulders while holding it in place with both hands.
2. While keeping your head up, back straight and your feet flush against the floor, slowly bend your knees and lower your body until your thighs are parallel to the ground.
3. Push yourself back to the starting position. Perform five sets of 8-10 repetitions preferably two times per week.

For more information about weight training for combat conditioning, see my War Machine book and War Machine II DVD program, available from my website at: www.sammyfranco.com

When confronted with a fighter who is about perform a takedown, be certain to adjust to his level of entry. Notice how the MMA fighter on the left has lowered his height (height change) prior to shooting in for the takedown.

"A solid and effective takedown will also require your MMA adversary to lower his base and get his hips under you. This means he will have to bend at his knees and back to lower his level of entry."

The Stiff-Arm Jam Technique

The stiff-arm jam is a very effective method of negating the destructive force of both the upper and mid body tackles. To perform the technique, simultaneously lower your base (height change to level of entry) and extend both of your arms forward. Both of your palms should make contact with the assailant's upper chest and shoulder. Be certain to pull your fingers back to avoid accidental sprains or breaks. Your objective is to instantaneously negate or "jam" the overwhelming force of the takedown.

In this photo, the man on the left performs the stiff-arm jam technique.

If the adversary attempts the upper body tackle, the palms of your hands should make contact on both sides of his chest region. If the grappler attempts a mid body tackle, lower your base and have your palms jam him at his shoulders. One more thing, it's critical that you remember to change your height to match your assailant's level of entry.

"It's critical that you always remember to change your height to match your assailant's level of entry.

In this photo, the fighter on the left attempts a takedown.

As the fighter moves in to tackle, the practitioner on the right immediately lowers his height to match the opponent's level of entry. He negates the MMA fighter's forward momentum with a stiff-arm jam to the upper chest region.

Once the stiff-arm jam negates the MMA fighter's momentum, the defender immediately moves in and engages the clinch position.

The defender then delivers a head butt strike to his assailant's nose.

The practitioner then follows up with a horizontal elbow strike.

"When performing the stiff-arm jam, be certain to pull your fingers back to avoid accidental sprains or breaks."

Integrating The Stiff-Arm Jam Into Flow Drills

To make the stiff arm jam a bit more instinctual in application, you can add it to a variety of flow drills. For example, you can add it to the Hubod exercise. See photo sequence on the next page:

STEP 1: In this photo, the two practitioners begin the hubod drill with the man on the left initiating a tight overhead strike. The man on the right block the hit.

STEP 2: After blocking the hit, the man on the right uses his right arm to redirect his partner's striking arm.

STEP 3: As the man on the right redirects his partners arm, he slaps it downward with his left hand.

STEP 4: The man on the right then strikes his partner with a tight overhead strike.

STEP 5: Next, the man on the left blocks his partner's hit.

STEP 6: Then redirects his partner's arm with his right hand.

STEP 7: Instead of slapping his partner's hand, the man on the left moves in with an upper body tackle. The man on the right immediately adapts with a stiff arm jam.

Deadly Force Situations: Webbing Against The Takedown

The Webbing technique was first introduced to the martial arts world in 2003 through our WidowMaker Program. This offensive based technique is utterly devastating and should only be used when deadly force is legally and morally justified.

At first glance, webbing looks like a reinforced palm heel strike. However, there is much more to it. It does require specific hand and arm articulation, proper body mechanics and correct timing. However, once mastered, Webbing™ will feel natural and will become an instinctual body weapon that can be deployed under the stress of a deadly criminal attack.

Ironically, Webbing is both an offensive and defensive technique that can immediately disable any opponent of any size. Interestingly enough, I termed this technique "Webbing" because your hands resemble a large web that wraps around the enemy's face.

The defender (right) intercepts the grappler's upper body tackle with a webbing strike to the chin. Notice how the grappler's momentum is negated by the strategic strike. Be certain that both of your hands are joined together as a single striking unit with your fingers jutting out to the sides of the grappler's face. Also, make sure that both of your arms extend and strike simultaneously.

What follows is a detailed breakdown of the proper body mechanics for effective Webbing™. Keep in mind that you must not forget to change your height to match your assailant's level of entry. Also, remember that proper Webbing body mechanics are executed in one explosive movement that should take less than one second to execute.

1. From a left lead (your left leg is forward) stance. Simultaneously overlap your left hand on top of your right hand. Your right thumb should be aligned under the 5th metacarpal of your left hand (see picture). Your right palm is the striking surface while your left reinforces the structural integrity of the strike. The left hand is also particularly important because it significantly reduces

the likelihood of a wrist or hand injury and it magnifies the power of the blow.

2. Once the hands are properly joined, forcefully extend both arms into the enemy's chin. Your elbows should also be slightly bent when impacting with the target. Do not completely lock your elbows. Unlike conventional punches, your body does not torque when launching the Webbing strike. Destructive power comes from synergistically utilizing your major muscle groups (i.e., back, chest, shoulders and triceps) accompanied with forward momentum.

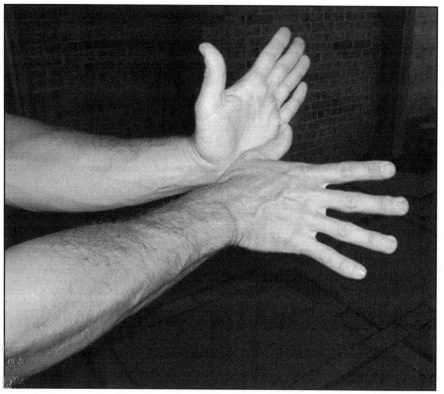

When performing a right hand Webbing strike, be certain your right thumb is aligned under the 5th metacarpal of your left hand.

3. The ideal trajectory of the Webbing blow should be approximately 45-degrees to the enemy's chin. Remember, you are trying to transmit shock

waves to the cerebellum and cerebral hemispheres of the assailant's brain. Once again, take into account that the angle of impact may change depending on the assailant's height change and level of entry. Make certain that both of your palms are perpendicular to the floor. This palm alignment will minimize finger sprains and maximize flush contact with the target.

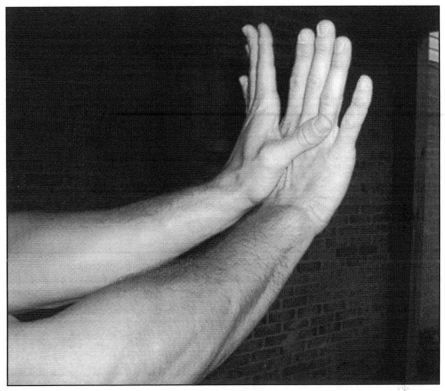

In this photo, the right palm is the striking surface while your left reinforces the structural integrity of the strike. To avoid finger jams or breaks, have your palms perpendicular to the ground.

4. You can launch the Webbing™ strike while remaining stationary, however forward momentum will increase the power exponentially. Forward momentum can be generated in one of two ways: the half step or the full step.

The Half Step - your lead foot moves forward approximately 24 inches, while the rear foot remains stationary.

The Full Step - move your front foot forward (approximately 24 inches) and then move your rear foot an equal distance.

5. Finally, once the two hands make solid contact with the target, allow both hands to split apart and engage the clinch.

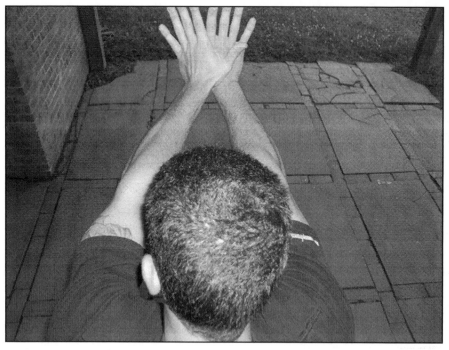

A birds-eye view of the webbing technique.

"Webbing can be deadly and should only be used in a situation where deadly force is legally and morally justified in the eyes of the law. It is your responsibility to comply with all local laws."

Sprawling Against The Tackle

Sprawling is used to counter both mid and lower body tackles and it is particularly effective against the single and double leg takedown. Essentially, this technique negates the penetration of the assailant's takedown by spreading your legs back and driving your hip into his head and shoulder. When sprawling, make certain to maintain steady pressure and square your hips as you arch them into the adversary.

Defending Against the Mid Body Tackle (Sprawling Counter)

STEP 1: In this photo, the MMA fighter (right) attempts a mid body tackle. The self-defense practitioner (left) immediately sprawls his legs back and drops his hips into the grappler's head and shoulders.

"Sprawling negates the penetration of the assailant's takedown by spreading your legs back and driving your hip into his head and shoulder."

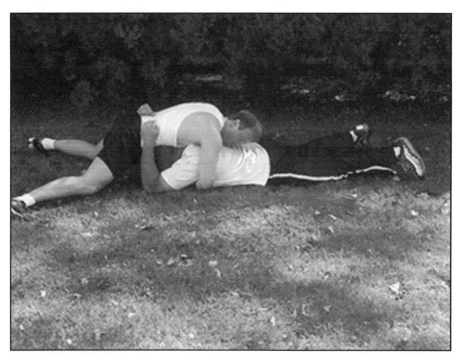

STEP 2: The defender (left) maintains steady pressure, which drives his opponent straight to the ground.

STEP 3: The defender (top) quickly pivots and rotates his body around the grappler's back.

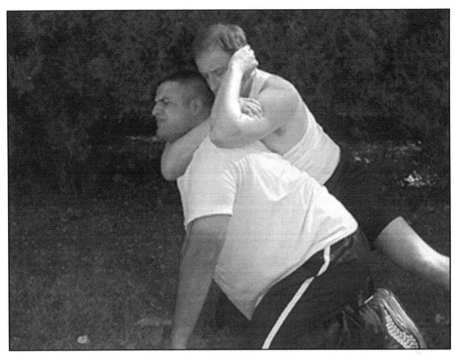

STEP 4: The practitioner executes a modified neck choke to incapacitate his mixed martial arts adversary.

CHAPTER SEVEN

When It Goes To The Ground

The Five Ground Fighting Positions

Despite all your training and preparation, there is always the possibility that a mixed martial artist will succeed in taking you to the ground. In fact, it's common knowledge that the majority of street fights will end up on the ground.

If a mixed martial artists does succeed in taking you to the ground, do not panic! Hope is not lost. Like all forms of combat, it is essential that you keep your head during the ground fight. Losing your temper or panicking when taken to the ground can cost you your life. However, "keeping your cool" will conserve energy and significantly reduce the possibility of tactical errors.

If you want to be truly prepared for a mixed martial artist you must make certain that you are equipped with the necessary techniques and skills necessary to handle a possible ground fight.

I have said repeatedly in many of my books and instructional DVDs, the longer a fight lasts, the greater your chances of injury or death. This is especially true in a ground fight. However, when ground fighting with an MMA fighter it's essential that you are prudent and that you do not rush a movement or technique. If you work too quickly, you might subject yourself to several risks and dangers.

"Despite all your training and preparation, there is always the possibility that a mixed martial artist will succeed in taking you to the ground."

For example, you can possibly lose your positional advantage, lose your balance or lose your leverage and expose yourself to a variety of counters by the assailant. More importantly, the strategic timing to the application of a ground fighting technique will be compromised and the technique will not work. The bottom line is work smartly!

Regardless of how proficient your striking arsenal may be, there is still a very strong possibility that the fight will go to the ground. Don't take any unnecessary risks. Make certain that you are equipped with the necessary knowledge, skills and attitude necessary to handle a ground fight.

Having said that, lets first look at the five ground fighting positions. Once I introduce them to you, we can move forward with specific escape techniques and counter attack tactics. The basic ground fighting positions are as follows:

- Mounted Position
- Perpendicular Mount Position
- Guard Position
- Chest to Back Position
- Opposite Pole Position

The Mounted Position

The Mount is a dominant position where the mixed martial artist is sitting on top of your torso or chest. The mounted position gives your adversary superior reach, gravitational punching power, range control and the ability to apply a wide variety of submission holds.

One of the primary strategies of the mounted position is to make the defender feel as uncomfortable as possible. The MMA fighter accomplishes this by dropping his bodyweight on his opponent (not the ground) and driving his hips through the body.

The MMA fighter might incorporate a grapevine with his mount. The grapevine is applied when he has either one (single leg grapevine) or both (double leg grapevine) of his feet hooked around your legs. This stabilization technique is called a grapevine because the body mechanics are similar to a grapevine entwined around a post.

The grapevine serves several strategic purposes in a ground fight. It bring about psychological panic for the uninitiated, causes pain in the thighs and hips and most importantly, it prevents you from bumping the grappler from the mounted position.

If the situation permits, sometimes a mixed martial artist will assume a "high mount" position. This is when he pulls himself up, sits on your chest and jams his knees deep into your armpits. Beware! The "high mount" position is ideal position for the adversary to launch striking blows.

A word of caution, if your assailant has established the mounted position during the ground fight, be certain NOT to offer him an extended arm. This can be dangerous for the some of the following reasons.

First, your elbows will lose strategic placement on his thighs, thus allowing him the opportunity to ride higher in the mounted position. A high mounted position will give him the ability to force you over and onto your stomach. Second, your assailant can perform a variety of holds and chokes like the biceps choke or the Japanese arm bar.

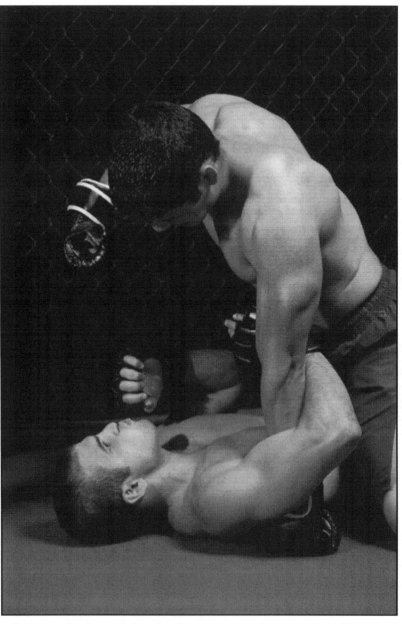

In this photo, a mixed martial artist demonstrates the top mounted position.

In this photo, the author demonstrates the mounted position. Keep in mind, striking the head from this dominant position can cause severe injury and possibly death to your adversary.

Keep Your Knees Up When Mounted

Whenever your assailant mounts you, it is important to instinctively keep your knees raised up. This is important for some of the following reasons:

- Raised knees bring your leg closer to the trapping foot position necessary to bump the assailant off you.
- Raised knees offer greater leverage and thrusting power than straight legs.
- Raised knees also facilitate mobility on the ground.

Perpendicular Mount Position

This is also known as the cross-body position or side mount. This is when the mixed martial artist is on top of you with his body running at a perpendicular angle to yours. The perpendicular mount actually has two variations: the "chest to chest" and "head to head" positions. When the MMA fighter assumes the chest-to-chest position, he will most likely keep his hips low and ride you at mid sternum to avoid any chances of you bridging and rolling to escape.

Pictured here, the perpendicular mount position.

The Guard Position

This is when the mixed martial artist is on his back with both his legs wrapped around your waist. Depending on whom you are fighting, some fighters will cross their legs at their ankles while others will do it at the knees (such as a figure four configuration).

Don't be fooled, although the guard is a defensive ground fighting position, a mixed martial artist can perform of wide variety of chokes and holds. Brazilian Jujitsu is well known for their combat proficiency from this ground fighting position.

Don't be fooled! If a mixed martial artist opens up his leg guard he could be performing a leg choke or reversal move.

In this photo, a female mixed martial artist performs an arm bar technique from the guard position.

Chest to Back Position

This is when a mixed martial artist has his chest against your back. It is the worst possible position you can find yourself in when ground fighting. One of the cardinal rules for ground fighting is, under no circumstances should you ever roll over onto your stomach and expose your back to the MMA fighter!

The chest to back position is dangerous because it is virtually impossible to defend yourself. Avoid exposing your back to your adversary at all costs! From this position, the opponent could easily choke you out or deliver a barrage of blows to your head, neck and spine.

In this photo, the fighter demonstrates the chest to back position. Also, notice that his leg guard is wrapped around his opponent's waist area. One of the cardinal rules for ground fighting is, under no circumstances should you ever roll over and expose your back to your opponent.

> *"The chest to back position is dangerous because it is virtually impossible to defend yourself. Avoid exposing your back to your adversary at all costs!*

Opposite Pole Position

The opposite pole position is created when both you and your opponent momentarily face opposite directions during the course of a ground fight. Believe it or not, this position occurs quite often in a ground struggle.

In this photo, a mixed martial artists performs an ankle lock from the opposite pole position.

Ground Fighting Escape Techniques

Now that we covered the various ground fighting positions, its time to learn some basic escape techniques. Let's start with escaping from the top mounted position.

Escaping From the Mounted Position (Technique #1)

In this photo, the CFA student (bottom) is being mounted by his opponent. The student traps his opponent's left arm and leg.

> *"Escaping from the top mounted position is one of the most important ground fighting skills you can master."*

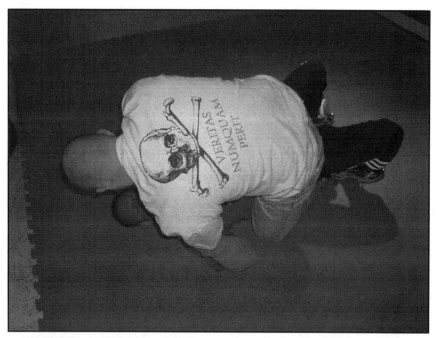

When the opponent's arms and leg are trapped, the student (bottom) thrusts his hips upwards and explosively turns to his right side. The mixed martial artist tumbles over.

Once the student has successfully bumped the grappler out of the mounted position, he ends up in his opponent's leg guard. Notice how the fighter (right) leans back when placed in his opponent's guard.

"Leaning back when in your opponent's leg guard is important for several reasons. First, it prevents your assailant from pulling you down and embracing you. Second, it offers you the range and angle to repeatedly strike the opponent's groin or strike his face if he decides to reach and grab you. Finally, it puts you into a position to escape from opponent's leg guard."

Escaping From the Mounted Position (Technique #2)

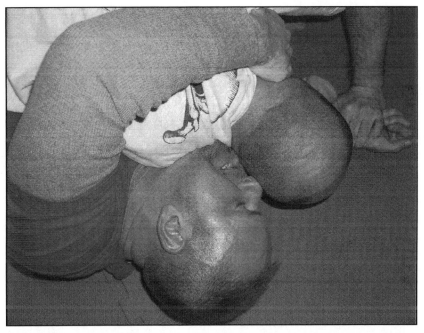

Another effective method of escaping from the top mounted position is to bite. In some circumstances biting a mixed martial artist's ear may be your only chance to escape from the mounted position. Remember, to only use biting tactics in deadly force situations where no other options exist.

Escaping from the Guard Position

In order to safely escape the grappler's leg guard, you must first weaken him with various strikes. The next series of photographs will illustrate this point.

Escaping From the Guard Position (Technique #1)

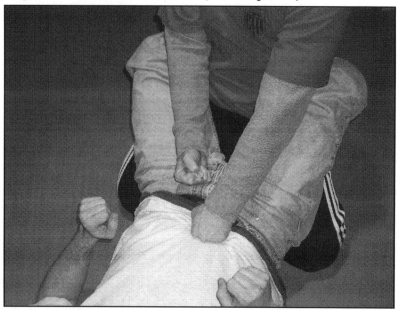

Hammering the MMA fighter's groin with your fists is another effective way of getting him to release his hold on you.

Escaping From the Guard Position (Technique #2)

If the situation warrants, you can counter the grappler with a throat crush. This is a deadly force technique so be certain that your actions are justified in the eyes of the law!

Escaping From the Guard Position (Technique #3)

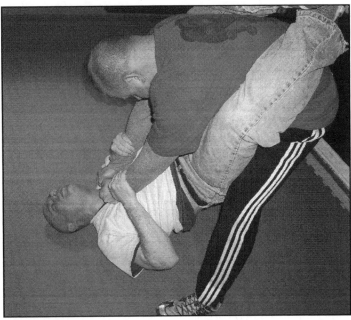

Another effective way of escaping from the opponent's leg guard is to simply lift him by the collar and repeatedly smash his skull into the pavement. Once again, this is a deadly force technique and should only be used in life and death situations. Be certain your actions are legally justified!

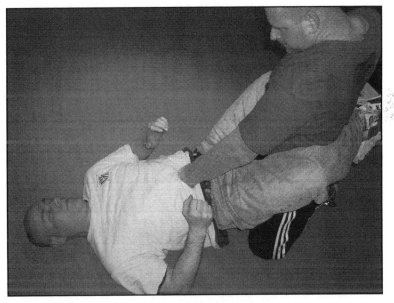

To prevent the grappler from pulling you down and embracing you, you can post your arm into his lower stomach. Notice how the student (right) does not expose his fingers to his adversary.

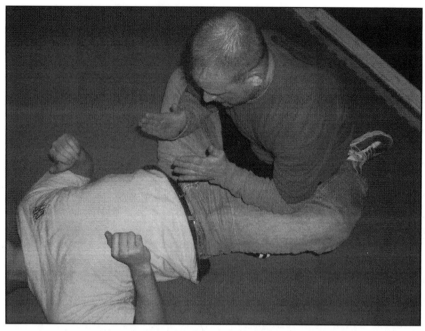

After you have weakened the grappler with strikes, you will a few seconds to escape from his guard. Begin, by leaning back and positioning both of your elbow points on the lower inside area of his thighs (by his knees).

Once your elbows are in position, aggressively push them out to the sides. The pain is excruciating and will cause the grappler to open his legs, allowing you to either escape of acquire a better position on the ground.

Escaping from the Perpendicular Mount Position

If you find yourself placed in a headlock from a perpendicular mount position, it's critical that your arms don't get trapped behind the opponent's back. In this photo, the student (bottom) demonstrates the wrong arm placement. From this position, there is very little that he can do to counter his opponent.

This is the correct hand placement when defending against a side headlock from a perpendicular mount position. Notice how the practitioner's hands are in front of the grappler's chest. This allows him to secure the "box frame" position against his opponent's throat.

Once the "box frame" is secured, the student (left) walks backwards and rocks the grappler backward into his legs where a leg choke counter awaits him.

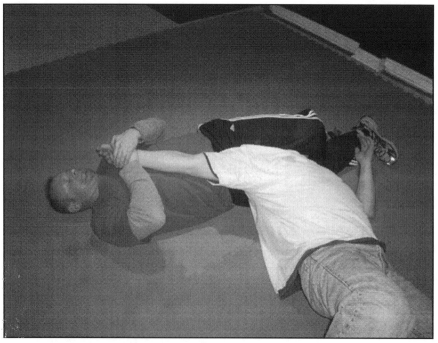

Once the leg choke is secure, the practitioner straightens his body out and finishes off the mixed martial artist with a straight-arm bar.

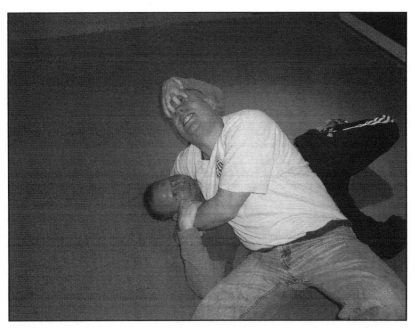

You can also drive your finger into your opponent's eyes and pull his head backwards allowing you a window of escape. Remember, attacking the eyes can permanently injure or blind your opponent so this technique should only be used when deadly force is warranted and justified.

Escaping from the Chest to Back Position

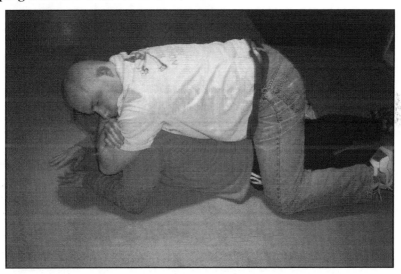

If a grappler has already applied a rear choke from a chest to back position, there is very little you can do to escape the situation. However, your only hope is to pretend that you have been choked out. If the opponent prematurely releases his choke, you can turn over and "sucker punch" him.

Ground Fighting Weapons

Now that you have a few escapes under your belt, it's time to get acquainted with your ground fighting weapons. You might not realize it but you do have a wide variety of ground fighting weapons at your disposal.

For reasons of simplicity, your ground fighting arsenal is divided into five different categories. They include the following: Immobilization Techniques, Locks, Chokes, Natural Body Weapons and Pain Compliance techniques.

- **Immobilization Techniques** - These are various techniques designed to immobilize your adversary.

- **Locks** - These are various submission holds designed to manipulate and injure your assailant's limbs.

- **Chokes** - These are various techniques designed to restrict your assailant's air and/or blood supply.

- **Natural Body Weapons** - These are various natural body weapons designed to inflict severe damage, (i.e., tight punches, hammer fists, biting, gouging, tearing, etc.).

- **Pain Compliance Techniques** - Also known as submission techniques. These are various techniques that create extreme pain for your MMA adversary.

Submission Techniques

Essentially, submission techniques include a wide variety of holds, chokes, and locks, designed to trap, pin and incapacitate your adversary in a ground fight. Like I said earlier, if you want to be truly prepared for the ground, make certain that you are well versed in this area of unarmed fighting. In this section, I will go over just a few important concepts.

Hand Grips for Submission Techniques

The foundation of your submission techniques are predicated on your handgrip. There are many different types of handgrips that you can use in a ground fight, however here are four that are worth mentioning.

Three Finger Grip

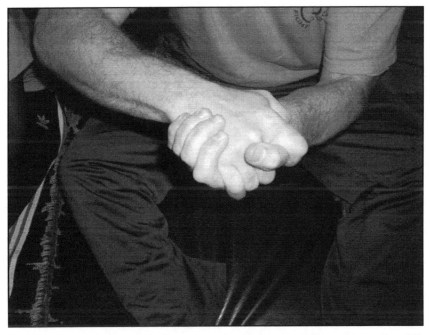

Join your hands together and place your thumb between the index and middle finger of your other hand. Now, clasp your hands together.

Knife Hand Grip

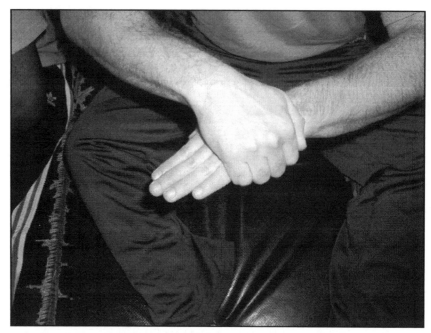

Join your hands together by grasping the knife edge of your other hand.

Wrist Grip

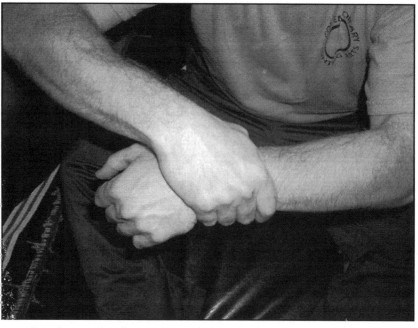

Join your hands together by grasping the wrist of your other hand.

Indian Grip

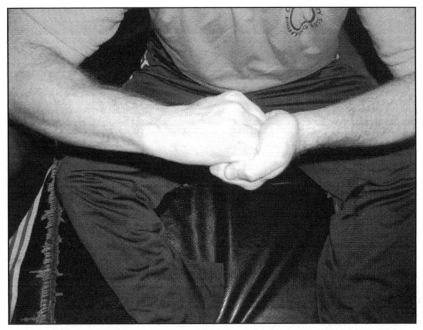

To perform the Indian grip, curl your fingers and join your hands together.

There are two handgrips you should avoid using during a ground fight. The full-hand and finger interlace grips. This full handgrip is combatively deficient because it separates your thumb too far apart from your other four fingers. This weakens the structural integrity of your grip thus allowing the grappler to escape your hold.

The finger interlace grip is dangerous because it dramatically inhibits your ability to switch to another grip or hold; it provides poor structural integrity and if your assailant can reach your fingers, he can squeeze them together, causing extreme pain and a possible finger dislocation.

A Word About Using Choking Techniques

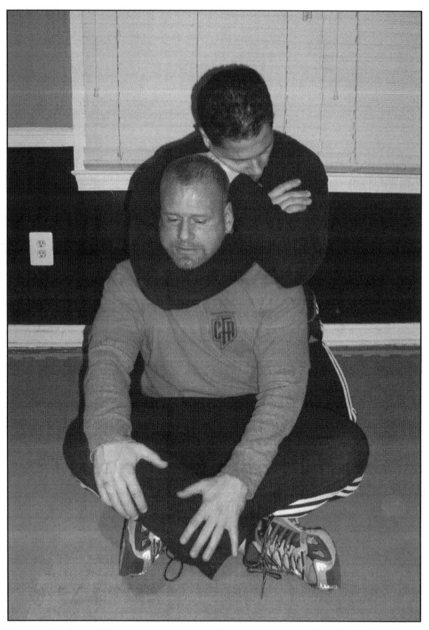

Chokes are designed to restrict your assailant's air and or blood supply. There are several chokes that can be applied in a ground fight. However, one of the most effective chokes you can employ is the rear naked choke. Warning! Choking technique can be deadly and should only be used when deadly force is justified in the eyes of the law.

I'm actually astonished by how many MMA schools will cavalierly teach their students choking techniques without first explaining the legal and medical implications. Be warned! All choking techniques are dangerous and can be deadly!

In this photo, a CFA student executes a brutal front choke from the mounted position. To apply this technique, follow these important steps: From the mounted position, place your right forearm behind the assailant's neck (blade side facing his neck). Then insert the web of your left hand into the crook of your right forearm and place the blade side of your left firearm into the assailant's windpipe. Next, compress and scissor both of your forearms into one another. Also, keep your base as low as possible and tuck your face away from the assailant. Make certain to employ the double leg grapevine when applying the forearm choke. This will prevent your adversary from bumping you out of the mounted position.

WARNING: The forearm choke can crush the assailant's windpipe, causing death. This ground fighting technique should only be used in life and death situations when lethal force is warranted and justified.

Body Weapon Tools

Your body weapons tools are another vital component of your ground fighting arsenal that can inflict severe damage to a seasoned mixed martial artist. Your body weapon tools include the following techniques:

- Tight linear punches
- Hammer fist strikes
- Biting
- Eye gouging and raking
- Fingers breaks
- Throat crushing
- Tearing flesh

Tight Linear Punches

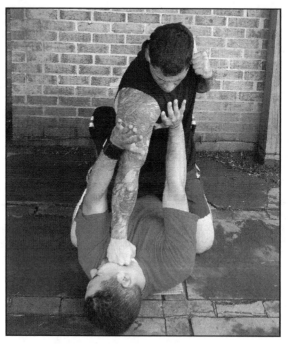

Once your balance is established in the mounted position, you can proceed with a vicious furry of strikes delivered to the opponent's face – this is know as pummeling. Punching from this position is extremely effective because you have the gravitational advantage and the grappler's head is flush against the floor (the floor functions as a stabilizer that concentrates your impact). The best blows for the pummel assault are tight linear punches, hammer fists, and in some cases elbow strikes. Pummeling from the top mounted position can be deadly. Always be certain that your actions are legally warranted and justified.

Breaking the Fingers

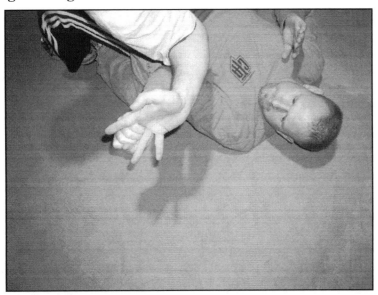

Every mixed martial artist needs his hands and fingers to fight. This is why it's one of the best targets to attack during a ground fight. Breaking your opponent's fingers is quick, efficient and can be employed while you are standing, kneeling and lying in various ground fighting positions.

Crushing the Throat

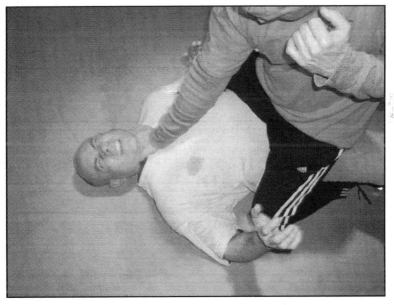

Crushing techniques work especially well when the opponent's body is anchored against the floor. Again, crushing should only be used in a life and death self defense situation where deadly force is justified in the eyes of the law.

"When faced with deadly force situations, you will want the quickest and most efficient method of neutralizing your adversary. One brutal "nuclear technique" is crushing. However, crushing the assailant's throat is not an easy task. It requires quick and exact digit placement, sufficient leverage accompanied with the vicious determination to destroy your assailant."

Biting the Opponent

Biting can be very effective when fighting on the floor. When biting, it's important to penetrate deep and hard with your molars and shake your head vigorously back and forth. Not only is biting effective on a physical level, it also transmits a strong psychological message to the assailant.

BEWARE! Biting should only be used as a last resort; you run the risk of contracting AIDS if your attacker is infected and you draw blood while biting him.

Gouging and Clawing the Eyes

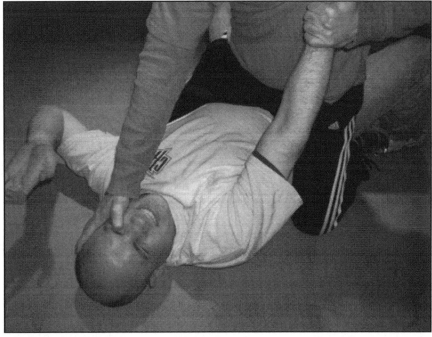

Driving your fingers into the opponent's eyes is another effective method of controlling a ground fight. However, be forewarned, some MMA fighters are very capable of ground fighting without the use of vision. This is why I encourage all of my students to regularly ground fight blindfolded.

Other Ground Fighting Tips

Mount the Opponent Immediately

If and when the street fight does go down to the ground, immediately try to mount your MMA adversary. Remember, the fighter who establishes the mounted position has a tremendous tactical advantage in the ground fight.

In Contemporary Fighting Arts, the mounted position is the "cockpit" from which to effectively finish off the opponent. The most important aspect of the mounted position is that it puts you in the best position to deliver a variety of destructive blows and submission holds, yet it is very difficult for your assailant to effectively counter or escape.

Whenever you are mounted on your assailant, it is equally important to "maintain" this position by keeping a low base. Here are a few key points to remember:

- **Relax your body** - a tense or rigid torso makes it easier for the assailant to throw you off.

- **Keep your center of gravity low and close to the opponent** - when applying submission holds from the mounted position always keep your chest married against the assailant's chest.

- **Be cognizant where you place your arms at all times** - they can be grabbed by the assailant and used as levers to bump you.

- **Grapevine his legs** - if possible keep your feet tucked under his thighs - this creates a "crazy glue" effect to the assailant.

- **Be patient** - if time permits, wait for your assailant to make his move of demise.

Use the Environment to Your Advantage

As I mentioned earlier in this book, a mixed martial artist is not accustomed to the street environment and will be out of his element when fighting in the real world. Remember to use this fact to your advantage.

For example, once you have established the mounted position, you should take advantage of your environment and use it to your advantage. Here are just a few good examples. Drive or smash the assailant's head or face into the pavement or curb of the street. This is often referred to as a "curbie".

If the situation presents itself, force your assailant's head under water, sand, snow, thick mud, a pile of wet leaves. Or shove your adversary's head or eyes into broken glass, thrust your assailant's eyes, or head into barb wire or razor wire, or maneuver your assailant's entire head into the pathway of moving machinery. WARNING: These examples of environmental exploitation should only be used in life and death encounters where lethal force is warranted and justified in the eyes of the law.

Never forget, the street is the ideal fighting environment for you and the worst place for a mixed martial artist.

When a Mixed Martial Artist Stands Above You

There might be a time when you are thrown to the ground and your opponent is standing above you. While an MMA fighter does have the tactical advantage, you can use the tailspin technique to get yourself out of trouble.

The tailspin is executed by first chambering one of your legs back (to launch a kick) then pivoting and rotating your body in the direction of the opponent. Quick pivoting can be accomplished by spinning on your butt while your elbows maintain your balance.

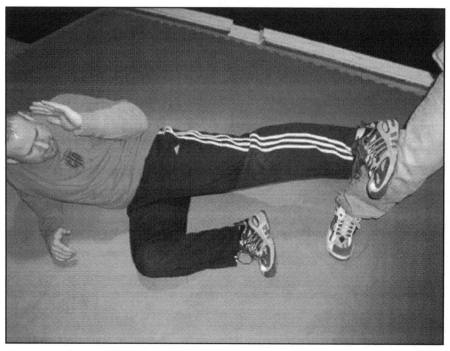

In this photo, the student uses the tailspin technique to launch his kick. Notice that he keeps his left arm up to protect his torso and face.

Be prudent when delivering kicking techniques during a ground fight. Avoid full chambering positions prior to delivering your kick. Not only will this telegraph your movements, but it will also allow your opponent to trap and control your lower body.

Know the Limitations of the Ground

Simply knowing the tactical limitations of ground fighting can also give you an edge over a mixed martial artist. Here are a few limitations that you should be aware of:

Multiple Assailants - since ground fighting requires maximal body entanglement, it is virtually impossible to fight multiple attackers. Avoid the ground at all costs if you are faced with m ore than one attacker!

Edged Weapons - it is often difficult to defend against knives and other edged weapons when locked up with your assailant on the ground.

Spectator Intervention - spectator intervention can occur when you are locked up in a ground fight.

Positional Asphyxia - when ground fighting a significantly heavier assailant, positional asphyxia can occur if you are not careful.

Terrain - the type of terrain you are ground fighting on can be extremely dangerous (i.e. broken glass, sharp metal, broken wood, etc.)

Environmental Dangers - your environment and immediate surrounding can harm you (i.e. heavy traffic, a cliff, the curb of the street, etc.)

Limited Mobility - you cannot move quickly or disengage the fight when you are locked up in a ground fight.

You'll Need to Train Regularly

To be truly prepared for a possible fight with a mixed martial artist, you must engage in rigorous and frequent ground fighting sessions with a trustworthy training partner. Once again, it's important to focus on employing many of the MMA foul techniques. Here's a brief list of important skills to focus on:

- Chokes
- Finger breaks
- Throat crushing

- Biting
- Pummeling
- Groin strikes
- Eye attacks
- Twisting and tearing flesh
- Hair pulling
- Head butts
- Applying CFA's <u>street oriented</u> submission holds
- Maintaining the mounted position
- Escaping the assailant's guard
- Escaping the mounted position
- Defending against pummeling
- Escaping from the side head lock
- Escapes from various submission holds and chokes
- Establishing the mounted position
- Establishing the perpendicular mount
- Maintaining the perpendicular mount

Due to the very nature of ground fighting training, there is always the possibility of injuries. Therefore, considerable attention must be given to safety. Here are a few tips and suggestions to keep injuries at a minimum. Warm up prior to ground fighting sessions; keep your fingernails well trimmed; don't wear jewelry during training sessions, practice with a training partner whom you can trust and who can control his techniques.

You should also experience what it is like to ground fight against different types of weapons. Experiment and see what it's like to grapple with edged weapons (use training knives only), sticks and bludgeons, and various types of makeshift weapons.

Try to ground fight while blind folded. This is important for the several reasons. First, it helps you develop a keen sense of kinesthetic awareness. Two, it helps prepare you to ground fight while visually handicapped. Three, it develops anatomical orientation allowing quick execution of submission techniques. Forth, it cultivates your tactile sight.

If you want to be exceptionally prepared for the ground fight, you'll need to experience what it's like to fight with only one arm. Find a trustworthy partner with whom you can work with (he can use both arms but you can only use one). This type of training is important for several reasons:

- It physically prepares you to fight while injured or handicapped.
- It psychologically prepares you to fight when injured or handicapped.
- It enhances you appendage awareness when ground fighting.
- It reinforces good survival tactics.
- It builds ground fighting confidence.

The unfortunate fact about grappling combat is that you may be faced with more than one adversary. Therefore, it's imperative that you experience what it's like to ground fight two assailants at the same time. This type of training can be conducted while you and your training partners are standing, kneeling or lying in the prone position. Remember, it's important that your training partners know how to work with you through the training session.

If you would like more detailed information about my submission techniques for street combat, please see my Submission Fighting For The Street DVD series, available from my web site at: www.sammyfranco.com

Notes

Glossary

The following terms are defined in the context of Contemporary Fighting Arts and its related concepts. In many instances, the definitions bear little resemblance to those found in a standard dictionary.

A

Accuracy - The precise or exact projection of force. Accuracy is also defined as the ability to execute a combative movement with precision and exactness.

Adaptability - The ability to physically and psychologically adjust to new or different conditions or circumstances of combat.

Advanced First Strike Tools - Offensive techniques that are specifically used when confronted with multiple opponents.

Aerobic Exercise - "With air." Exercise that elevates the heart rate to a training level for a prolonged period of time, usually 30 minutes.

Affective Preparedness – One of the three components of preparedness. Affective preparedness means being emotionally, philosophically and spiritually prepared for the strains of combat. (see cognitive preparedness and psychomotor preparedness.)
Aggression - Hostile and injurious behavior directed toward a person.

Aggressive Response – One of the three possible counters when assaulted by a grab, choke or hold from a standing position. Aggressive response requires you to counter the enemy with destructive blows and strikes. (See moderate response and passive response.)

Aggressive Hand Positioning - Placement of hands so as to imply aggressive or hostile intentions.

Agility - An attribute of combat. One's ability to move his or her body quickly and gracefully.

Amalgamation - A scientific process of uniting or merging.

Ambidextrous - The ability to perform with equal facility on both the right and left sides of the body.

Anabolic Steroids – synthetic chemical compounds that resemble the male sex hormone called testosterone. This performance-enhancing drug is known to increase lean muscle mass, strength and endurance.

Analysis and Integration - One of the five elements of CFA's mental component. This is the painstaking process of breaking down various elements, concepts, sciences, and disciplines into their atomic parts, and then methodically and strategically analyzing, experimenting, and drastically modifying the information so that it fulfills three combative requirements: efficiency, effectiveness and safety. Only then is it finally integrated into the CFA system.

Anatomical Striking Targets - The various anatomical body targets that can be struck and which are especially vulnerable to potential harm. They include: the eyes, temple, nose, chin, back of neck, front of neck, solar plexus, ribs, groin, thighs, knees, shins, and instep.

Anti-Grappling techniques – Techniques and maneuvers specifically designed to fight a grappler in a street fight.

Assailant - A person who threatens or attacks another person.

Assault - The willful attempt or threat to inflict injury upon the person of another.

Assault and Battery - The unlawful touching of another person without justification.

Assessment - The process of rapidly gathering, analyzing, and accurately evaluating information in terms of threat and danger. You can assess people, places, actions, and objects.

Attack - Offensive action designed to physically control, injure, or kill another person.

Attitude – One of the three factors that determine who wins a street fight. Attitude means being emotionally, philosophically and spiritually liberated from societal and religious mores. (See skills and knowledge.)

Attributes of Combat - The physical, mental, and spiritual qualities that enhance combat skills and tactics.

Awareness - Perception or knowledge of people, places, actions, and objects. (In CFA there are three categories of tactical awareness: criminal awareness, situational awareness, and self-awareness.)

B

Balance - One's ability to maintain equilibrium while stationary or moving.

Blading the Body - Strategically positioning your body at a 45-degree angle.

Blitz and Disengage - A style of sparring whereby a fighter moves into a range of combat, unleashes a strategic compound attack, and then quickly disengages to a safe distance. Of all sparring methodologies, the Blitz and Disengage closely resembles a real street fight.

Block - A defensive tool designed to intercept the assailant's attack by placing a non-vital target between the assailant's strike and your vital body target.

Body Composition - The ratio of fat to lean body tissue.
Body Language - Nonverbal communication through posture, gestures, and facial expressions.

Body Mechanics - Technically precise body movement during the execution of a body weapon, defensive technique, or other fighting maneuver.

Body Tackle – A tackle that occurs when your opponent haphazardly rushes forward and plows his body into yours.

Body Weapon - (also known as tool). One of the various body parts that can be used to strike or otherwise injure or kill a criminal assailant.

Bums Rush – A slang term for upper body tackle.

Burn Out – A negative emotional state acquired by physically over training. Some symptoms include: illness, boredom, anxiety, disinterest in training, and general sluggishness.

C

Cadence - Coordinating tempo and rhythm to establish a timing pattern of movement.

Cardiorespiratory Conditioning - The component of physical fitness that deals with the heart, lungs, and circulatory system.

Centerline - An imaginary vertical line that divides your body in half and which contains many of your vital anatomical targets.

Choke Holds – A particular hold that impairs the flow of blood or oxygen to the brain.

Circular Movement - Movements that follow the direction of a curve.

Clinching - Strategically locking up with the adversary while you are standing.

Close Quarter Combat - One of the three ranges of knife and bludgeon combat. At this distance, you can strike, slash, or stab your assailant with a variety of close-quarter techniques.

Cognitive Development - One of the five elements of CFA's mental component. The process of developing and enhancing your fighting skills through specific mental exercises and techniques. (See analysis and integration, killer instinct, philosophy and strategic/tactical development.)

Cognitive Exercises - Various mental exercises used to enhance fighting skills and tactics.

Cognitive Preparedness – One of the three components of preparedness. Cognitive Preparedness means being equipped with the strategic, concepts, principles and general knowledge of combat. (See affective preparedness and psychomotor preparedness.)

Combat Oriented Training – Training that is specifically related to the harsh realities of both armed and unarmed combat. (see ritual oriented training and sport oriented training.)

Combative Arts - The various arts of war. (See martial arts.)

Combative Attributes - (See attributes of combat.)

Combative Fitness - A state characterized by cardiorespiratory and muscular/ skeletal conditioning, as well as proper body composition.

Combative Mentality - (also known as the killer instinct). A combative state of mind necessary for fighting. (see killer instinct.)

Combat Ranges - The various ranges of unarmed combat.

Combative Utility - The quality of condition of being combatively useful.

Combination(s) - (See compound attack.)

Common Peroneal Nerve - A pressure point area located approximately four to six inches above the knee on the midline of the outside of the thigh.

Composure - A combative attribute. Composure is a quiet and focused mind set that enables you to acquire your combative agenda.

Compound Attack - One of the five conventional methods of attack. Two or more body weapons launched in strategic succession whereby the fighter overwhelms his assailant with a flurry of full speed, full force blows.

Conditioning Training - A CFA training methodology requiring the practitioner to deliver a variety of offensive and defensive combinations for a four minute period (See proficiency training and street training.)

Contact Evasion - Physically moving or manipulating your body to avoid being tackled by the adversary.

Contemporary Fighting Arts® (CFA) - A modern martial art and self-defense system made up of three parts: physical, mental , and spiritual.

Conventional Ground Fighting Tools - Specific ground fighting techniques designed to control, restrain and temporarily incapacitate your adversary. Some conventional ground fighting tactics include: submission holds, locks, certain choking techniques, and specific striking techniques.

Coordination - A physical attribute characterized by the ability to perform a technique or movement with efficiency, balance, and accuracy.

Counterattack - Offensive action made to counter an assailant's initial attack.

Courage - A combative attribute. The state of mind and spirit that enables a fighter to face danger and vicissitudes with confidence, resolution, and bravery.

Courageousness - (See courage.)

Creative Monohydrate - A tasteless and odorless, white powder that mimics some of the effects as anabolic steroids. Creatine is a safe body building product that can benefit anyone who wants to increase their strength, endurance and lean muscle mass.

Criminal Awareness - One of the three categories of CFA awareness. It involves a general understanding and knowledge of the nature and dynamics of a criminal's motivations, mentalities, methods, and capabilities to perpetrate violent crime. (See situational awareness and self-awareness.)

Criminal Justice - The study of criminal law and the procedures associated with its enforcement.

Criminology - The scientific study of crime and criminals.

Cross Stepping - The process of crossing one foot in front or behind the other when moving.

Crushing Tactics - Nuclear grappling range techniques designed to crush the assailant's anatomical targets.

D

Deadly Force - Weapons or techniques that may result in imminent, unconsciousness, permanent disfigurement, or death.

Deception - A combative attribute. A stratagem whereby you delude your assailant.

Decisiveness - A combative attribute. The ability to follow a tactical course of action that is unwavering and focused.

Defense - The ability to strategically thwart an assailant's attack (armed or unarmed).

Defensive Flow - A progression of continuous defensive responses.

Defensive Mentality - A defensive mind-set.

Defensive Reaction Time - The elapsed time between an assailant's physical attack and your defensive response to that attack (See offensive reaction time.)

Demeanor - One of the essential factors to consider when assessing a threatening individual. A person's outward behavior.

Diet - A life-style of healthy eating.

Disingenuous Vocalization - The strategic and deceptive utilization of words to successfully launch a pre-emptive strike at your adversary.

Distancing - The ability to quickly understand spatial relationships and how they relate to combat.

Distractionary Tactics - Various verbal and physical tactics designed to distract your adversary.

Double-End Bag – A small leather ball suspended in the air by bungee cord which develops striking accuracy, speed, timing, eye-hand coordination, footwork and overall defensive skills.

Double Leg Takedown – A takedown that occurs when your opponent shoots for both of your legs to forces you to the ground.

E

Ectomorph – One of the three somatotypes. A body type characterized by a high degree of slenderness, angularity and fragility. (See endomorph and mesomorph.)

Effectiveness - One of the three criteria for a CFA body weapon, technique, tactic or maneuver. It means the ability to produce a desired effect (See efficiency and safety.)

Efficiency - One of the three criteria for a CFA body weapon, technique, tactic or maneuver. It means the ability to reach an objective quickly and economically (see effectiveness and safety.)

Emotionless - A combative attribute. Being temporarily devoid of human feeling.

Endomorph – One of the three somatotypes. A body type characterized by a high degree of roundness, softness, and body fat. (See ectomorph and mesomorph.)

Evasion - A defensive maneuver that allows you to strategically maneuver your body away from the assailant's strike.

Evasive Sidestepping - Evasive footwork where the practitioner moves to either the right or left side.

Evasiveness - A combative attribute. The ability of avoid threat or danger.

Excessive Force - An amount of force that exceeds the need for a particular event and is unjustified in the eyes of the law.

Experimentation - The painstaking process of testing a combative hypothesis or theory.

Explosiveness - A combative attribute that is characterized by a sudden outburst of violent energy.

F

Fear - A strong and unpleasant emotion caused by the anticipation or awareness of threat or danger. There are three stages of fear in order of intensity: Fright, Panic, and Terror. (See fright, panic, and terror.)

Feeder - A skilled technician who manipulates the focus mitts.

Femoral Nerve - A pressure point area located approximately six inches above the knee on the inside of the thigh.

Fighting Stance - One of the different types of stances used in CFA's system. A strategic posture you can assume when face-to-face with an unarmed assailant (s). The fighting stance is generally used after you have launched your first strike tool.

Fight-or-Flight Syndrome - A response of the sympathetic nervous system to a fearful and threatening situation, during which it prepares your body to either fight or flee from the perceived danger.

Finesse - A combative attribute. The ability to skillfully execute a movement or a series of movements with grace and refinement.

First Strike - Proactive force used to interrupt the initial stages of an assault before it becomes a self-defense situation.

First Strike Principle (FSP) - A CFA principle which states that when physical danger is imminent and you have no other tactical option but to fight back, you should strike first, strike fast, and strike with authority and keep the pressure on.

First Strike Stance - One of the different types of stances used in CFA's system. A strategic posture used prior to initiating a first strike.

First Strike Tools - Specific offensive tools designed to initiate a pre-emptive strike against your adversary.

Fisted blows – Hand blows delivered with a clenched fist.

Five Tactical Options – The five strategic responses you can make in a self-defense situation, listed in order or increasing level of resistance: comply, escape, de-escalate, assert, and fight back.

Flexibility - The muscles' ability to move through maximum natural ranges (See muscular/skeletal conditioning.)

Focus Mitts – Durable leather hands mitts used to develop and sharpen offensive and defensive skills.

Footwork - Quick, economical steps performed on the balls of the feet while you are relaxed, alert, and balanced. Footwork is structured around four general movements: forward, backward, right, and left.

Fright - The first stage of fear; quick and sudden fear (See panic and terror.)

G

Gi – Japanese term for a martial art uniform.

Grappler – A combatant who prefers to fight at close quarter range. His objective is to either grab, clinch, tackle, throw or wrestle you to the ground where he can establish a superior position and neutralize you with a myriad of submission holds and chokes.

Grappling Range - One of the three ranges of unarmed combat. Grappling range is the closest distance of unarmed combat from which you can employ a wide variety of close-quarter tools and techniques. The grappling range of unarmed combat is also divided into two different planes: vertical (standing) and horizontal (ground fighting). (See kicking range and punching range.)

Grappling Range Tools - The various body tools and techniques that are employed in the grappling range of unarmed combat, including head butts; biting, tearing, clawing, crushing, and gouging tactics; foot stomps, horizontal, vertical, and diagonal elbow strikes, vertical and diagonal knee strikes, chokes, strangles, joint locks, and holds. (See punching range tools and kicking range tools.)

Ground Fighting - Fighting that takes place on the ground. (Also known as the horizontal grappling plane).

Guard – (also known as hand guard) A fighter's hand positioning.

Guard Position – (also known as leg guard or scissors hold). A ground fighting position when fighter is on his back with his opponent between his legs.

H

Hand Positioning - (See guard.)

Hand Wraps – Long strips of cotton that are wrapped around the hands and wrists for greater protection.

Haymaker - A wild and telegraphed swing of the arms executed by an unskilled fighter.

Head-Hunter - A fighter who primarily attacks the head.

Heavy Bag - A large cylindrical shaped bag that is used to develop kicking, punching or striking power.

High-Line Kick - One of the two different classifications of a kick. A kick that is directed to targets above an assailant's waist level. (See low-line kick.)

Hip Fusing - A full contact drill that teaches a fighter to "stand his ground" and overcome the fear of exchanging blows with a stronger opponent. This exercise is performed by having two fighters connected to each other (by a 3-foot chain), forcing them to fight in the punching range of unarmed combat.

Histrionics - The field of theatrics or acting.

Hook Kick - A circular kick that can be delivered in both kicking and punching ranges.

Hook Punch - A circular punch that can be delivered in both the punching and grappling ranges.

I

Impact Power - Destructive force generated by mass and velocity.

Impact Training - A training exercise that develops pain tolerance.

Incapacitate - To disable an assailant by rendering him unconscious or damaging his bones, joints or organs.

Initiative - Making the first offensive move in combat.

Inside Position – The area between both the opponent's arms where he has the greatest amount of control.

Intent - One of the essential factors to consider when assessing a threatening individual. The assailant's purpose or motive (See demeanor, positioning, range, and weapon capability.)

Intuition - The innate ability to know or sense something without the use of rational thought.

J

Jiu-jitsu – Translates to "soft/pliable". Jiu-jitsu is a martial art developed in feudal Japan that emphasizes throws, joint locks and weapons training.

Joint Lock - A grappling range technique that immobilizes the assailant's joint.

Judo - Translates to "gentle/soft way". Judo is an Olympic sport which originated in Japan.

K

Kick - A sudden, forceful strike with the foot.

Kicking Range - One of the three ranges of unarmed combat. Kicking range is the furthest distance of unarmed combat wherein you use your legs to strike an assailant. (See grappling range and punching range.)

Kicking Range Tools - The various body weapons employed in the kicking range of unarmed combat, including side kicks, push kicks, hook kicks, and vertical kicks.

Killer Instinct - A cold, primal mentality that surges to your consciousness and turns you into a vicious fighter.

Kinesics - The study of nonlinguistic body movement communications (i.e., eye movement, shrugs, facial gestures, etc.).

Kinesiology - The study of principles and mechanics of human movement.

Kinesthetic Perception - The ability to accurately feel your body during the execution of a particular movement.

Knowledge – One of the three factors that determine who will a street fight. Knowledge means knowing and understanding how to fight. (See skills and attitude.)

L

Lead Side -The side of the body that faces an assailant.

Leg Guard – (See guard position.)

Linear Movement - Movements that follow the path of a straight line.

Low Maintenance Tool - Offensive and defensive tools that require the least amount of training and practice to maintain proficiency. Low maintenance tools generally do not require preliminary stretching.

Low-Line Kick - One of the two different classifications of a kick. A kick that is directed to targets below the assailant's waist level. (See high-line kick.)

Lock - (See joint lock.)

M

Maneuver - To manipulate into a strategically desired position.

MAP – An acronym that stands forModerate, Aggressive and Passive. MAP provides the practitioner with three possible responses to various grabs, chokes and holds that occur from a standing position. (See aggressive response, moderate response, and passive response.)

Martial arts - The "arts of war".

Masking – The process of concealing your true feelings from your opponent by manipulating and managing your body language.

Mechanics - (See body mechanics.)

Mental Attributes - The various cognitive qualities that enhance your fighting skills.

Mental Component - One of the three vital components of the CFA system. The mental component includes the cerebral aspects of fighting including the Killer Instinct, Strategic & Tactical Development, Analysis & Integration, Philosophy and Cognitive Development (See physical component and spiritual component.)

Mesomorph – One of the three somatotypes. A body type classified by a high degree of muscularity and strength. The mesomorph possess the ideal physique for unarmed combat. (See ectomorph and endomorph.)

Mobility - A combative attribute. The ability to move your body quickly and freely while balanced. (See footwork.)

Moderate Response – One of the three possible counters when assaulted by a grab, choke or hold from a standing position. Moderate response requires you to counter your opponent with a control and restraint (submission hold). (See aggressive response and passive response.)

Modern Martial Art - A pragmatic combat art that has evolved to meet the demands and characteristics of the present time.

Mounted Position - A dominant ground fighting position where a fighter straddles his opponent.

Muscular Endurance - The muscles' ability to perform the same motion or task repeatedly for a prolonged period of time.

Muscular Flexibility - The muscles' ability to move through maximum natural ranges.

Muscular Strength - The maximum force that can be exerted by a particular muscle or muscle group against resistance.

Muscular/Skeletal Conditioning - An element of physical fitness that entails muscular strength, endurance, and flexibility.

N

Naked choke - A throat choke executed from the chest to back position. This secure choke is executed with two hands and it can be performed while standing, kneeling and ground fighting with the opponent.

Neutralize - (See incapacitate.)

Neutral Zone - The distance outside of the kicking range from which neither the practitioner nor the assailant can touch the other.

No Holds Barred Competition (NHB) – A sport competition with few rules.

Non aggressive Physiology - Strategic body language used prior to initiating a first strike.

Non telegraphic Movement - Body mechanics or movements that do not inform an assailant of your intentions.

Nuclear Ground Fighting Tools - Specific grappling range tools designed to inflict immediate and irreversible damage. Some nuclear tools and tactics include: (1) Biting tactics; (2) Tearing tactics; (3) Crushing tactics; (4) Continuous Choking tactics; (5) Gouging techniques; (6) Raking tactics; (7) And all striking techniques.

O

Offense - The armed and unarmed means and methods of attacking a criminal assailant.

Offensive Flow - Continuous offensive movements (kicks, blows, and strikes) with unbroken continuity that ultimately neutralize or terminate the opponent. (See compound attack.)

Offensive Reaction Time (ORT) - The elapsed time between target selection and target impaction.

One-Mindedness - A state of deep concentration wherein you are free from all distractions (internal and external).

Ostrich Defense – One of the biggest mistakes one can make when defending against an opponent. When the practitioner will look away from that which he fears (i.e. punches, kicks and strikes). His mentality is, "If I can't see it, it can't hurt me."

P

Pain Tolerance - Your ability to physically and psychologically withstand pain.

Panic - The second stage of fear; overpowering fear (See fright and terror.)

Pankration – meaning "complete strength". A Greek martial art that utilizes kicks, punches, strikes , grappling and submission holds. It is said that the first recorded date of a Pankration match was 648 B.C.

Parry - A defensive technique; a quick, forceful slap that redirects an assailant's linear attack. There are two types of parries: horizontal and vertical.

Passive Response – One of the three possible counters when assaulted by a grab, choke or hold from a standing position. Passive response requires you to nullify the assault without injuring your adversary. (See aggressive response and moderate response.)

Patience - A combative attribute. The ability to endure and tolerate difficulty.

Perception - Interpretation of vital information acquired from your senses when faced with a potentially threatening situation.

Philosophical Resolution - The act of analyzing and answering various questions concerning the use of violence in defense of yourself and others.

Philosophy - One of the five aspects of CFA's mental component. A deep state of introspection whereby you methodically resolve critical questions concerning the use of force in defense of yourself or others.

Physical Attributes - The numerous physical qualities that enhance your combative skills and abilities.

Physical Component - One of the three vital components of the CFA system. The physical component includes the physical aspects of fighting including Physical Fitness, Weapon/Technique Mastery, and Combative Attributes   (See mental component and spiritual component.)

Physical Conditioning - (See combative fitness.)

Physical Fitness - (See combative fitness.)

Positional Asphyxia -   The arrangement, placement or positioning of your opponent's body which interrupts your breathing and causes unconsciousness or possible death.

Positioning - The spatial relationship of the assailant to the assailed person in terms of target exposure, escape, angle of attack, and various other strategic considerations.

Post Traumatic Syndrome (PTS) - A group of symptoms that may occur in the aftermath of a violent confrontation with a criminal assailant. Common symptoms of Post Traumatic Syndrome include denial, shock, fear, anger, severe depression, sleeping and eating disorders, societal withdrawal, and paranoia.

Power - A physical attribute of armed and unarmed combat. The amount of force you can generate when striking an anatomical target.

Power Generators – Specific points on your body which generate impact power. There are three anatomical power generators: shoulders, hips, and feet.

Precision - (See accuracy.)

Pre-emptive Strike - (See first strike.)

Premise - An axiom, concept, rule or any other valid reason to modify or go beyond that which has been established.

Preparedness – A state of being ready for combat. There are three components of preparedness: affective preparedness, cognitive preparedness and psychomotor preparedness.

Proficiency Training - A CFA training methodology requiring the practitioner to execute a specific body weapon, technique, maneuver or tactic over and over for a prescribed number or repetitions (See conditioning training and street training.)

Proxemics - The study of the nature and effect of man's personal space.

Proximity - The ability to maintain a strategically safe distance from a threatening individual.

Pseudospeciation - A combative attribute. The tendency to assign subhuman and inferior qualities to a threatening assailant.

Psychological Conditioning - The process of conditioning the mind for the horrors and rigors of real combat.

Psychomotor Preparedness – One of the three components of preparedness. Psychomotor preparedness means possessing all of the physical skills and attributes necessary to defeat a formidable adversary. (See affective preparedness and cognitive preradeness.)
Punch - A quick, forceful strike of the fists.

Punching Range - One of the three ranges of unarmed combat. Punching range is the mid range of unarmed combat from which the fighter uses his hands to strike his assailant. (See kicking range and grappling range.)

Punching Range Tools - The various body weapons that are employed in the punching range of unarmed combat, including finger jabs, palm heel strikes, rear cross, knife hand strikes, horizontal and shovel hooks, uppercuts, and hammer fist strikes. (See grappling range tools and kicking range tools.)

Q

Qualities of Combat - (See attributes of combat.)

R

Range - The spatial relationship between a fighter and a threatening assailant.

Range Deficiency - The inability to effectively fight and defend in all ranges (armed and unarmed) of combat.

Range Manipulation - A combative attribute. The strategic manipulation of combat ranges.

Range Proficiency - A combative attribute. The ability to effectively fight and defend in all ranges (armed and unarmed) of combat.

Ranges of Engagement - (See combat ranges.)

Ranges of Unarmed Combat - The three distances a fighter might physically engage with an assailant while involved in unarmed combat: kicking range, punching range, and grappling range.

Reaction Dynamics - The assailant's physical response or reaction to a particular tool, technique, or weapon after initial contact is made.

Reaction Time - The elapsed time between a stimulus and the response to that particular stimulus (See offensive reaction time and defensive reaction time.)

Rear Cross - A straight punch delivered from the rear hand that crosses from right to left (if in a left stance) or left to right (if in a right stance).

Rear Side - The side of the body furthest from the assailant (See lead side.)

Reasonable Force - That degree of force which is not excessive for a particular event and which is appropriate in protecting yourself or others.

Refinement - The strategic and methodical process of improving or perfecting.

Relocation Principle – (also known as Relocating) A street fighting tactic that requires you to immediately move to a new location (usually by flanking your adversary) after delivering a compound attack.

Repetition - Performing a single movement, exercise, strike or action continuously for a specific period.

Research - A scientific investigation or inquiry.

Rhythm - Movements characterized by the natural ebb and flow of related elements.

Ritual Oriented Training – Formalized training that is conducted without intrinsic purpose. (See combat oriented training and sport oriented training.)

S

Safety - One of the three criteria for a CFA body weapon, technique, maneuver or tactic. It means the that the tool, technique, maneuver or tactic provides the least amount of danger and risk for the practitioner (See efficiency and effectiveness.)

Sambo – A Russian martial art predicated on wrestling and Judo

Scissors Hold – (See guard position.)

Self-Awareness - One of the three categories of CFA awareness. Knowing and understanding yourself. This includes aspects of yourself which may provoke criminal violence and which will promote a proper and strong reaction to an attack. (See criminal awareness and situational awareness.)

Self-Confidence - Having trust and faith in yourself.

Self-Enlightenment - The state of knowing your capabilities, limitations, character traits, feelings, general attributes, and motivations (See self-awareness.)

Set - A term used to describe a grouping of repetitions.

Shadow Fighting - A CFA training exercise used to develop and refine your tools, techniques, and attributes of armed and unarmed combat.

Shoot - An explosive forward movement (generally low level) while grabbing the opponent's legs with the sole objective of taking a person to the ground.

Shootfighting – A Japanese combat sport that combines kick boxing, wrestling and Jiu-Jitsu.

Shooting Range – The range at which a knowledgeable grappler will most likely attempt a takedown. Most likely within his arms reach (punching range).

Situational Awareness - One of the three categories of CFA awareness. A state of being totally alert to your immediate surroundings, including people, places, objects, and actions. (See criminal awareness and self-awareness.)

Skeletal Alignment - The proper alignment or arrangement of your body. Skeletal Alignment maximizes the structural integrity of striking tools.

Skills – One of the three factors that determine who will win a street fight. Skills refers to psychomotor proficiency with the tools and techniques of combat. (See Attitude and Knowledge.)

Slipping - A defensive maneuver that permits you to avoid an assailant's linear blow without stepping out of range. Slipping can be accomplished by quickly snapping the head and upper torso sideways (right or left) to avoid the blow.

Snap Back - A defensive maneuver that permits you to avoid an assailant's linear and circular blow without stepping out of range. The snap back can be accomplished by quickly snapping the head backwards to avoid the assailant's blow.

Somatotypes – A method of classifying human body types or builds into three different categories: endomorph, mesomorph and ectomorph. (See endomorph, mesomorph, and ectomorph.)

Sparring – A training exercise where two (or more) fighters fight each other while wearing protective equipment.

Speed - A physical attribute of armed and unarmed combat. The rate or a measure of the rapid rate of motion.

Spiritual Component - One of the three vital components of the CFA system. The spiritual component includes the metaphysical issues and aspects of existence (See physical component and mental component.)

Sport Oriented Training – Training that is geared for competition that is governed by a set of rules. (See combat oriented training and ritual oriented training.)

Sprawling – A grappling technique used to counter a double or single leg takedown.

Square-Off - To be face-to-face with a hostile or threatening assailant who is about to attack you.

Stance - One of the many strategic postures that you assume prior to or during armed or unarmed combat.

Stand Up Fighter – This term generally refers to a combatant who primarily remains standing when fighting.

Stick Fighting – Fighting that takes place with either one or two sticks.

Stiff Arm Jam – A defensive technique used to negate the destructive force of both the upper and mid body tackles.

Strategic Positioning - Tactically positioning yourself to either escape, move behind a barrier, or use a makeshift weapon.

Strategic/Tactical development - One of the five elements of CFA's mental component.

Strategy - A carefully planned method of achieving your goal of engaging an assailant under advantageous conditions.

Street Fight - A spontaneous and violent confrontation between two or more individuals wherein no rules apply.

Street Fighter - An unorthodox combatant who has no formal training. His combative skills and tactics are usually developed in the street by the process of trial and error.

Street Training - A CFA training methodology requiring the practitioner to deliver explosive compound attacks for ten to twenty seconds (See conditioning training and proficiency training.)

Strength Training - The process of developing muscular strength through systematic application of progressive resistance.

Striking Art - A combat art that relies predominantly on striking techniques to neutralize or terminate a criminal attacker.

Striking Shield - A rectangular shaped shield constructed or foam and vinyl used to develop power in most of your kicks, punches and strikes.

Striking Tool - A natural body weapon that impacts with the assailant's anatomical target.

Strong Side - The strongest and most coordinated side of your body.

Structure - A definite and organized pattern.

Style - The distinct manner in which a fighter executes or performs his combat skills.

Stylistic Integration - The purposeful and scientific collection of tools and techniques from various disciplines, which are strategically integrated and dramatically altered to meet three essential criteria: efficiency, effectiveness, and combative safety.

Submission Hold – (also known as control and restraint techniques). Many of the locks and holds that create sufficient pain to cause the adversary to submit.

Submission Technique - Includes all locks, bars, and holds that cause sufficient pain to cause the adversary to submit.

System - The unification of principles, philosophies, rules, strategies, methodologies, tools, and techniques or a particular method of combat.

T

Tactic - The skill of using the available means to achieve an end.

Takedown - A move or maneuver in combat in which a standing fighter is forced to the floor.

Target Awareness - A combative attribute which encompasses 5 strategic principles: target orientation, target recognition, target selection, target impaction, and target exploitation.

Target Exploitation - A combative attribute. The strategic maximization of your assailant's reaction dynamics during a fight. Target Exploitation can be applied in both armed and unarmed encounters.

Target Impaction - The successful striking of the appropriate anatomical target.

Target Orientation - A combative attribute. Having a workable knowledge of the assailant's anatomical targets.

Target Recognition - The ability to immediately recognize appropriate anatomical targets during an emergency self-defense situation.

Target Selection - The process of mentally selecting the appropriate anatomical target for your self-defense situation. This is predicated on certain factors, including proper force response, assailant's positioning and range.

Target Stare - A form of telegraphing whereby you stare at the anatomical target you intend to strike.

Target Zones - The three areas which an assailant's anatomical targets are located. (See zone one, zone two and zone three.)

Technique - A systematic procedure by which a task is accomplished.

Telegraphic Cognizance - A combative attribute. The ability to recognize both verbal and non-verbal signs of aggression or assault.

Telegraphing - Unintentionally making your intentions known to your adversary.

Tempo - The speed or rate at which you speak.

Terminate - The act of killing.

Terror - The third stage of fear; defined as overpowering fear (See fright and panic.)

Timing - A physical and mental attribute or armed and unarmed combat. Your ability to execute a movement at the optimum moment.

Tone - The overall quality or character of your voice.

Tool - (See body weapon.)

Traditional Martial Arts - Any martial art that fails to evolve and change to meet the demands and characteristics of its present environment.

Traditional Style/System - (See traditional martial art.)

Training Drills - The various exercises and drills aimed at perfecting combat skills, attributes, and tactics.

Trapfighting – The American version of shootfighting.

U

Unified Mind - A mind free and clear of distractions and focused on the combative situation.

Use of Force Response - A combative attribute. Selecting the appropriate level of force for a particular emergency self-defense situation.

V

Vale Tudo – A Brazilian grappling sport that originated from street fighting.

Viciousness - A combative attribute. The propensity to be extremely violent and destructive often characterized by intense savagery.

Violence - The intentional utilization of physical force to coerce, injure, cripple, or kill.

Visualization – Also known as Mental Visualization or Mental Imagery. The purposeful formation of mental images and scenarios in the mind's eye.

W

Warm-up - A series of mild exercises, stretches, and movement designed to prepare you for more intense exercise.

Weak Side - The weakest and most uncoordinated side of your body.

Weapon and Technique Mastery - A component of CFA's physical component. The kinesthetic and psychomotor development of a weapon or combative technique.

Weapon Capability - An assailant's ability to use and attack with a particular weapon.

Y

Yell - A loud and aggressive scream or shout used for various strategic reasons.

Z

Zone One - Anatomical targets related to your senses, including the eyes, temple, nose, chin, and back of neck.

Zone Three - Anatomical targets related to your mobility, including thighs, knees, shins, and instep.

Zone Two - Anatomical targets related to your breathing, including front of neck, solar plexus, ribs, and groin.

ABOUT SAMMY FRANCO

Sammy Franco is one of the world's foremost authorities on armed and unarmed combat. Highly regarded as a leading innovator in combat sciences, Mr. Franco was one of the premier pioneers in the field of "reality-based" self defense.

Convinced of the limited usefulness of martial arts in real street fighting situations, Mr. Franco believes in the theory that the best way to change traditional thinking is to make antiquated ideas obsolete through superior methodology. His innovative ideas have made a significant contribution to changing the thinking of many in the field about how people can best defend themselves against vicious and formidable adversaries.

Sammy Franco is perhaps best known as the founder and creator of Contemporary Fighting Arts (CFA), a state-of-the-art offensive-based combat system that is specifically designed for real-world self-defense. CFA is a sophisticated and practical system of self-defense, designed specifically to provide efficient and effective methods to avoid, defuse, confront, and neutralize both armed and unarmed attackers.

After studying and training in numerous martial art systems and related disciplines and acquiring extensive firsthand experience from real "street" combat, Mr. Franco developed his first system, known as Analytical Street Fighting. This system, which was one of the first practical "street fighting" martial arts, employed an unrestrained reality-based training methodology known as Simulated Street Fighting. Analytical Street Fighting served as the foundation for the fundamental principles of Contemporary Fighting Arts and Mr. Franco's teaching methodology.

CFA also draws from the concepts and principles of numerous sciences and disciplines, including police and military science, criminal justice, criminology, sociology, human psychology, philosophy, histrionics, kinesics, proxemics, kinesiology, emergency medicine, crisis management, and human anatomy.

Sammy Franco has frequently been featured in martial art magazines, newspapers, and appeared on numerous radio and television programs. Mr. Franco has also authored numerous books, magazine articles and editorials, and has developed a popular library of instructional DVDs and workout music. As a matter of fact, his book Street Lethal was one of the first books ever published on the subject of reality based self defense. His other books include Killer Instinct, When Seconds Count, 1001 Street Fighting Secrets, First Strike, The Bigger They Are – The Harder They Fall, War Machine, War Craft, Ground War, Warrior Wisdom, Gun Safety Handbook and Heavy Bag Training.

Sammy Franco's experience and credibility in the combat science is unequaled. One of his many accomplishments in this field includes the fact that he has earned the ranking of a Law Enforcement Master Instructor, and has designed, implemented, and taught officer survival training to the United States Border Patrol (USBP). He instructs members of the US Secret Service, Military Special Forces, Washington DC Police Department, Montgomery County, Maryland Deputy Sheriffs, and the US Library of Congress Police. Sammy Franco is also a member of the prestigious International Law Enforcement Educators and Trainers Association (ILEETA) as well as the American Society of Law Enforcement Trainers (ASLET) and he is listed in the "Who's Who Director of Law Enforcement Instructors."

Sammy Franco is a nationally certified Law Enforcement Instructor in the following curricula: PR-24 Side-Handle Baton, Police Arrest and Control Procedures, Police Personal Weapons Tactics, Police Power Handcuffing Methods, Police Oleoresin Capsicum Aerosol Training (OCAT), Police Weapon Retention and Disarming Methods, Police Edged Weapon Countermeasures and "Use of Force" Assessment and Response Methods.

Mr. Franco is also a National Rifle Association (NRA) instructor who specializes in firearm safety, personal protection and advanced combat pistol shooting.

Mr. Franco holds a Bachelor of Arts degree in Criminal Justice from the University of Maryland. He is a regularly featured speaker at a number of professional conferences, and conducts dynamic and enlightening seminars on numerous aspects of self defense and personal protection.

Mr. Franco has instructed thousands of students in his career, including instruction on street fighting, grappling and ground fighting, boxing and kickboxing, knife combat, multiple opponent survival skills, stick fighting, and firearms training. Having lived through street violence himself, Mr. Franco's goal is not its glorification, but to help people free themselves from violence and its costly price.

For more information about Mr. Franco and his Contemporary Fighting Arts system, you can visit his websites at:

www.sammyfranco.com and www.contemporaryfightingarts.com

~Finis~

46544853R00109

Made in the USA
Lexington, KY
07 November 2015